The

Am

The Handbook for
Americans

~

OUT OF MANY, ONE

A Book to Benefit the People

hatherleigh

》》 hatherleigh

Text Copyright © 2018 Hatherleigh Press

No part of this book may be reproduced, stored in a
retrieval system, or transmitted, in any form or by any
means, electronic or otherwise, without written permission
from the Publisher.

Hatherleigh Press is committed to preserving and
protecting the natural resources of the Earth.
Environmentally responsible and sustainable practices
are embraced within the company's mission statement.

Hatherleigh Press is a member of the Publishers Earth
Alliance, committed to preserving and protecting
the natural resources of the planet while developing
a sustainable business model for the book
publishing industry.

Library of Congress Cataloging-in-Publication Data is
available upon request.

ISBN: 978-1-57826-759-0

The Handbook for Americans is available for bulk
purchase, special promotions, and premiums. For
information on reselling and special purchase
opportunities, call 1-800-528-2550 and ask for the
Special Sales Manager.

10 9 8 7 6 5 4 3 2 1

Printed in the United States

The Handbook for
Americans

~

TOO OFTEN WE AS AMERICAN CITIZENS take a "wait and see" attitude towards events. We go about our daily lives, assuming and hoping that someone else will take care of things. Someone in City Hall, or the state capital, or in Washington. Well, we are that "someone else." And we need to take responsibility now.

It was Robert F. Kennedy who said, "The future does not belong to those who are content with today, apathetic toward common problems and their fellow man alike, timid and fearful in the face of bold projects and new ideas. Rather, it will belong to those who can blend passion, reason, and courage in a personal commitment to the ideals of American society."

Passion, reason, and courage: these are the lifeblood of American citizenship.

—Andrew Flach, *Publisher*

11 PRINCIPLES FOR
EVERYDAY CITIZENSHIP

HERE IS A LIST OF ELEVEN THINGS you can do to participate immediately as a citizen of the United States. Eleven simple things you can do to build what President Franklin Delano Roosevelt called "a greater, a more stable and a more tolerant America." Because the ultimate success of our democracy rests upon the individual citizens who make up this great Nation.

Vote. By participating in elections at the local, state and national level, we make our opinions heard. Understand the issues. Learn as much as you can about the candidates. Vote responsibly.

Stay informed. Read newspapers, magazines, blogs. Talk to your friends, co-workers, neighbors. Go online and read current Bills before Congress. An educated American is an empowered citizen.

Exercise your right to free speech. When we articulately and intelligently state our opinions, popular or not, we truly live up to the hopes and dreams of the Founding Fathers. Freedom of speech is an extraordinary right.

Support American businesses. When we buy products labeled "Made in USA," we are supporting our economy and creating jobs for our fellow citizens.

Support Americans in need. Katrina. Ike. Devastating forest fires. Our neighbors need us. Help your fellow Americans. Donate your time, services, or money to those less fortunate than you.

Use your time meaningfully and wisely. Volunteer for local charities. Help out at the local school or nursing home. Organize a neighborhood clean-up. Let's all do what we can to support each other.

Reread our founding documents. The principles laid out in the Declaration of Independence, Constitution, and the Bill of Rights are timeless and essential. This country's Founders envisioned a future we are living out today—and we can turn to these documents whenever our democratic institutions and expectations are challenged and need to be reinvigorated.

Look to the past for perspective. Our Nation's history is rich with moments when strength and resilience transcended hardship and adversity. Look to the lives of our great leaders, Presidents, and citizens for inspiration.

Teach the next generation. Like anything else, enlightened patriotism comes from education, not ignorance. Teach the children about the special rights and responsibilities we share as Americans, and how they can exercise those rights. Set the example by being a good citizen.

Enjoy and protect America's natural resources. Conserve. Recycle. Help clean up a river or plant a tree. Our democracy deserves a home as beautiful as its ideals.

Above all else: Bet on Good. Believe in America. Believe that together we can forge a better future and better ways of doing things. Believe it, then do it.

TABLE OF CONTENTS

THE AMERICAN'S CREED

I BELIEVE IN THE UNITED STATES OF AMERICA as a government of the people, by the people, for the people; whose just powers are derived from the consent of the governed, a democracy in a republic, a sovereign Nation of many sovereign States; a perfect union, one and inseparable; established upon those principles of freedom, equality, justice, and humanity for which American patriots sacrificed their lives and fortunes.

I therefore believe it is my duty to my country to love it, to support its Constitution, to obey its laws, to respect its flag, and to defend it against all enemies.

— WRITTEN 1917,
accepted by the United States
House of Representatives
on April 3, 1918

I

What it Means
to Be an American

"I like to see a man proud of the place in which he lives. I like to see a man live so that his place will be proud of him."

—ABRAHAM LINCOLN (1809–1865)
Sixteenth U.S. President

OUR RIGHTS AS AMERICANS are protected by the Declaration of Independence and the Constitution, the documents that founded this country. These great documents guarantee the basic freedoms and protections that are the right of every American, regardless of background, culture, or religion.

But the definition of American is not set in stone. It is a living, breathing identity, one we shape daily through our actions, at home and abroad. Freedom is one of many American principles which must be upheld and defended every day. We do that by participating actively in the political process and by being an active member of society and our communities.

How we will honor the words and intentions of our Founders while moving into the future is the true test of being an American.

We are America.

"Every good citizen makes his country's honor his own, and cherishes it not only as precious but as sacred."

—ANDREW JACKSON (1767–1845)
*Seventh President
of the United States*

A BRIEF HISTORY
OF THE UNITED STATES

AMERICA'S HISTORY IS RICH with stories of determination and accomplishment in the face of challenge. With every trouble and every triumph, America has become stronger and wiser as a nation.

Discovery. The land mass that makes up the United States was originally home to a diverse population of native peoples. In 1493, Christopher Columbus became the first European to set foot on this sprawling continent when he landed in Puerto Rico on his second expedition to the New World. The Spanish, who were the first Europeans to colonize the New World, would establish "New Spain" from Florida to California over the next hundred years.

The French occupied North America as well, to the north and south of New Spain. Jacques Cartier led an expedition exploring the St. Lawrence in 1534, and, by 1712, New France stretched from Newfoundland and the Hudson Bay (in what is now Canada) all the way down to Louisiana. The French colonies included: Canada, Acadia, Hudson Bay, Newfoundland, and Louisiana.

English settlement of the New World was more haphazard than Spanish and French colonization. During the first decades of the seventeenth century, settlements were established by trading companies and religious groups (like the Puritans at Massachusetts Bay Colony). Some settlements were specifically set up as penal colonies.

The French and Indian War (1754–1763). This war rearranged the map of the future United States. With the defeat of the French and Spanish, Britain laid claim to the New World east of the Mississippi. More and more colonialists from Britain crossed the ocean to make a life in this new land. But Britain, under the rule of King George III, maintained a firm grip on the lives of the colonialists, carefully controlling trade in the new thirteen colonies.

By 1775, the colonialists had decided to break free from British rule. The battles of Lexington and Concord soon followed, setting the stage for what would later come to be known as the American Revolution. In early July, 1776, while throngs of British soldiers were arriving in New York, ready to battle General George Washington's outnumbered Continental Army, the Founding Fathers met in Philadelphia to draft the Declaration of Independence. During this pivotal moment in history, the Declaration of Independence became more than just a document of freedom; it also rang out as a battle cry for the Continental Army. With their defeat in 1782, the British ceded all lands west of the Mississippi, and a new nation was born.

The Constitution. In the summer of 1787, delegates gathered at the Constitutional Convention in Philadelphia to draft a Constitution that would establish the ground rules for the new American government. That same summer, the Northwest Ordinance was passed, establishing claim to the Northwest Territory. In 1788, the First Congress of the United States presented twelve amendments to the new Constitution to the states for ratification. Ten of these were approved and now make up the Bill of Rights. In 1789, the President of the Constitutional Convention, General George Washington, was unanimously elected by the Electoral College to become the first President of the United States. A new nation, made up of only 12 states, including recently adopted North Carolina, was born.

As Washington began his term of office and a new century dawned, the country continued to grow. Territories in the Northwest Territory, the south, and the East Coast were admitted as states, with full representation in Congress. In addition to Rhode Island (1790), Vermont (1791), and Kentucky (1792), Tennessee joined the U.S. in 1796, to carve out land in the Southwest Territory. In 1803, Ohio was admitted to the United States, making it the seventeenth state.

Expansion. Also in 1803, the United States purchased some 828,000 square miles of land west of the Mississippi (stretching from the Gulf of Mexico to the Canadian border) from France for the equivalent of twenty-three million dollars. Curious about just what these newly acquired lands looked like, President Jefferson dispatched Captain Meriwether Lewis, a White House aide, and William Clark, a veteran military man and adventurer, to explore these vast new holdings. The Lewis and Clark expedition followed the Missouri River to the Pacific Ocean. After two years of exploration, Lewis and Clark returned to the East with detailed maps and information on an amazing variety of plants and animals.

In addition to discovery, the new century also brought conflict. Since 1793, Britain had been at war with France, and the United States unwillingly became embroiled in the conflict when Britain started restricting American overseas trade and forcibly recruiting American sailors into the British Navy. This soon led to war. Not long after James Madison was elected second President, in 1812, fighting began. The war ranged from Canada and the Great Lakes to the Chesapeake Bay and continued until 1815. It was during this war, known as the War of 1812 that British troops stormed Washington, D.C. and occupied the capitol for 26 hours. After stealing food and souvenirs from the White House, they set fire to the building on August 24, 1814. Some have called this war the "second war of independence."

The Missouri Compromise. After the war, America continued its expansion. However, as different states were added to the

Union, the nation's stance on slavery became more and more of an issue. In an attempt to solve the problem, Congress balanced the number of "slave" and "free" states by alternating their admission. For example, after Indiana was admitted to the Union as a free state in 1816, Mississippi was brought in as a slave state in 1817. However, when Congress considered admitting Missouri as a slave state, shifting the balance in favor of the pro-slavery camp, debate ensued. The Missouri Compromise of 1820, which admitted Missouri as a slave state but prohibited slavery in the territory surrounding Missouri, and admitted Maine as a free state, settled the dispute. But this would not be the last time Congress would rule on the issue of slavery, an issue which would be a source of nationwide conflict for years to come.

The Trail of Tears. The growth of the United States also brought much bloodshed. In 1838, the United States Government, backed by Army troops, forcibly removed the Cherokee people from their native lands in Georgia to the territory of Oklahoma to make room for white settlers and gold seekers. The Cherokee were forced to march over 1200 miles. Over 4000 Cherokee, weakened by hunger and disease, died on what is known as the Trail of Tears. The United States Government expelled entire Native American populations, including the Choctaw, the Seminole, the Creek, and the Chickasaw, with other forced marches.

There were other flashpoints as well. Texas, which was by law part of Mexico, was annexed by the United States in 1845 as a slave state, setting off the Mexican-American War of 1846–48. With its defeat, Mexico ceded to the United States a huge swath of western land which would eventually become California, Nevada, Utah, and parts of Colorado, Arizona, New Mexico, and Wyoming. Much of this area was settled by Americans seeking a new life and new land—and sometimes riches. The discovery of gold in the foothills of California in 1848 sent on a "gold rush" out West in search of fortune. Elsewhere in the country, pioneers blazed trails from the Midwest to the West, including the Oregon Trail (Missouri to Oregon) and the Mormon Trail (Illinois to Utah).

The Civil War. By 1861, there were a total of 33 states in the U.S. Yet the country was far from united regarding the matter of slavery. The 15 slave states (Alabama, Arkansas, Delaware, Florida, Georgia, Kentucky, Louisiana, Maryland, Mississippi, Missouri, North Carolina, South Carolina, Tennessee, Texas, and Virginia) relied on the institution of slavery to uphold their way of life, economic interests, and political clout. When three free states were admitted to the Union in quick succession (Minnesota in 1858, Oregon in 1859, and Kansas in 1861) thus giving the free states a legislative advantage, the balance Congress had tried so desperately to maintain was overturned, and the slave states soon took aggressive action. The first shots of the Civil War were fired at Fort Sumter, South Carolina, in 1861, when the newly formed Confederate States of America (made up of the slave states South Carolina, Mississippi, Florida, Alabama, Georgia, Louisiana, and Texas) began battle and an attempt to secede, or separate, from the rest of the U.S.

Lincoln and the Emancipation Proclamation. Abraham Lincoln, elected President in 1860, would lead the country through four years of the brutal Civil War, which raged across the country and took over

600,000 American lives (a loss greater than all American casualties from the Revolutionary War to the Vietnam War combined). One of Lincoln's greatest legacies is the Emancipation Proclamation of 1863, which freed slaves in the Confederate states and led to the end of the War. Part of Lincoln's motivation for the Proclamation was to encourage newly freed slaves to join the Union forces, but the Emancipation Proclamation was also a benchmark on America's road to racial equality. The Proclamation greatly contributed to the North's cause, with over 200,000 black men joining the Northern army and leading to the North's victory. Two years later, on April 9, 1865, Confederate general Robert E. Lee surrendered General Ulysses S. Grant of the North at Appomattox Court House, Virginia. Lincoln was shot less than a week later by Confederate sympathizer John Wilkes Booth at Ford's Theater.

Aftermath of the War. Although the Civil War was over, the United States was far from unified. In the wake of the Civil War, three constitutional amendments were adopted in an attempt to address slavery and its legacy: the Thirteenth, which abolished slavery; the

Fourteenth, which extended federal legal protections equally to citizens regardless of race; and the Fifteenth, which ended racial restrictions on voting. But the tensions within the country remained. During the postwar period, Southern states established a complex set of local laws, known as "Jim Crow" laws, to uphold segregation and thwart racial equality. Many of these laws would remain on the books until the mid-twentieth century.

The period after the Civil War brought unprecedented technological and economic growth for the United States. The first commercial oil well was dug in 1859 in Titusville, Pennsylvania. By the 1880s, oil was widely sought for heating and lighting needs, and became a staple in most households. With the invention of the combustion engine, oil became an invaluable resource for vehicles of transportation. At the same time, processes for manufacturing inexpensive steel were developed. Industry boomed. Buildings, reinforced with steel girders, soared skywards, and the Brooklyn Bridge opened to traffic in 1883.

Economic Boom. America's economic boom attracted immigrants from around the world. In 1886, the Statue of Liberty, a symbol of America's promise of freedom, was dedicated by President Grover Cleveland. Soon thereafter, in 1890, President Harrison opened the Oklahoma territory to settlers. As a result, Americans and European immigrants alike jumped at the chance for property and prosperity. In 1892, Ellis Island was opened to process the waves of European immigrants who crossed the ocean for the chance to begin a new life in the United States.

The United States' economic power meant new international status as well. In 1898, after battles against Spain in Cuba, Guam and the Philippines, the Treaty of Paris granted new territories to the US in the Pacific and Caribbean. America's might now reached across oceans as well as the continent.

"The Gilded Age" and the early 1900s. Fortunes were made and lost during America's great financial boom at the end of the 19th century. It was Mark Twain who termed this period as "The Gilded Age," in response to the abundance of material goods and new wealth. The boom saw a country surging with energy and invention. The automobile, phonograph, kinetoscope, public utility lines, Coca Cola—these inventions and countless others made

America a leader in innovation, and helped to shape the modern world we live in today.

At the same time, there were calls for conservation and protection for the country's natural resources. In 1906, President Theodore Roosevelt began designating parcels of land with historic or natural significance as national monuments. This would lead to the creation of the National Park Service in 1916.

World War I. America's international stature was tested by its entrance into the First World War. An aging system of allies, along with far-reaching colonial ambitions and intense commercial competition between Britain and Germany, sparked the conflict in 1914. After remaining neutral, the United States entered the war in April, 1916, when German U-boat (submarine) attacks threatened America's shipping industry. Four million men were drafted. At times, American troops were arriving in Europe at the rate of 10,000 a day. The war provided the United States with new markets dedicated to the development and manufacturing of military supplies.

The United States also benefited from the financial and political aftermath of the Great War as it was able to erase national debt from foreign investments and embraced their renewed status as a world leader. It was also a time of social change. The passage of the 18th Amendment, or Prohibition, was a victory for the temperance movement, while the 19th Amendment, granting women the right to vote, recognized women's growing role in the workplace and society.

The Depression. This financial boom was, unfortunately, short-lived. The economic miracle of the early twentieth century collapsed in 1929 with the stock market crash. Banks were shut down, businesses failed, and millions were thrown out of work. Soup kitchens and bread lines were common sights in many towns and cities. Recognizing that the federal government had the resources and authority to step in and prop up the ailing nation, President Franklin Delano Roosevelt instituted his "New Deal," a program of public assistance that helped pull Americans back on their feet. The Social Security program, farm subsidies and certain economic reforms are all remnants of Roosevelt's Depression-era "call to arms."

World War II. The outbreak of World War II helped reignite America's manufacturing base. After years of economic deprivation,

German Chancellor Adolf Hitler launched a campaign to expand and solidify Germany's territory. In the Far East, Japan was also exercising its territorial ambitions. As in World War I, the United States remained neutral at the beginning of the conflict. But when the Japanese attacked Pearl Harbor in 1941, the United States entered the war. In many ways America was a country to be reckoned with, backed both by industrial might and a ready, willing and able population of young men to fill the ranks of the army, navy, and marines. America's unique position as a world power was made clear at war's end, when Harry Truman ordered the use of the new atomic bomb on the Japanese cities of Hiroshima and Nagasaki, and authorized the Marshall Plan for the recovery of a devastated Europe.

Post-War Boom. The post-war boom of the 1950s and '60s led to economic prosperity and consumer comfort. Television ownership jumped to 30 million in the mid-1950s, enabling Americans to witness Neil Armstrong's moon landing from their very own homes. At the same time, the United States faced challenges from overseas and growing conflict at home. Abroad, the United States was locked in a nuclear showdown with its Cold War rival, the Soviet Union. At home, the Civil Rights movement pushed for the roll-back of Jim Crow laws and the recognition of equal rights for all American citizens. Feder-ally-mandated school desegregation led to bat-tles over states rights, revisiting many of the tensions first exposed in the Civil War, and, ultimately, led to the Civil Rights Act of 1964, which outlawed racial segregation in schools, public places, and places of employment.

Tragic Assasinations. But America faced even more struggles, and they would prove to be unlike any its citizens had ever seen. On November 22, 1963, President John F. Kennedy was shot while driving through Dallas, an event that shocked a nation. The assassination act not only took the life of one of America's most beloved Presidents, but also shocked an entire country unaccustomed to fatal violence brought against its own gov-ernment, by its own citizens. More horrifying moments followed, with the shooting of Mar-tin Luther King, Jr., in April, 1968, and the assassination of Robert Kennedy, Jr., JFK's younger brother and New York Senator, less than three months later.

Vietnam. Meanwhile, since 1959, the United States had been waging abroad with North Vietnam. Again, television brought the bloodshed home, saturating the country with more images of violence. In 1965, President Johnson escalated the war, increasing the number of American troops deployed from 3,500 to 200,000 in less than a year. As more ground fighting led to tremendous loss of life and American men were drafted, voices speaking out against the war were in full swing. When, in 1970, four anti-war students at Kent State University were shot by U.S. troops, many Americans who had been undecided about the country's involvement in the war became completely outraged against their own government, and demanded that the U.S. withdraw. The late 1960s was a time of great rebellion, mass gatherings, and riots, and a culture of dissent manifested itself in new music, fashion, and literature. By the end of the war, in 1975, the cultural mood of the country had forever shifted away from an unwavering trust in the government.

The Reagan Years. The election of President Ronald Reagan in 1981 ushered in an era of deregulation and financial boom. Wall

Street thrived and the benefits of the boom were evident in an unprecedented explosion of consumer goods and services. The average American household overflowed with the latest trendy items in fashion, music, and entertainment.

The Clinton and Bush Administrations. The industrial infrastructure which provided the muscle behind America's almost century-long ascendance was aging, however. Manufacturers looked overseas for cheaper workers and facilities. The American economy shifted slowly towards services and away from manufacturing. The Clinton and Bush administrations presided over this sea-change in the American economy.

A New Century. The new millennium dawned on a United States whose economic and cultural global reach was irrefutable. That global reach made the United States a scapegoat and target for extremist groups of all types. The terrorist attacks on September 11, 2001, were a pointed attack on America's way of life that occurred on our own shores and took the lives of thousands of innocent civilians. Across the country, Americans felt grief, outrage, and fear. In Washington, a new era in America's foreign relations unfolded. The Bush Administration responded to 9/11 by invading Afghanistan (the seat of Al Qaeda's operations) and Iraq. It increased military spending, reorganized its national security apparatus, and launched a new campaign against global terrorism. The resulting drain on the United States economy, estimated at billions of dollars each month, has forced reassessments of the government's ability to meet its domestic responsibilities, and the federal government has been called upon to respond to serious financial crises.

Today, America faces challenges that, although they may be new, affect all of us in much the same way that past struggles shaped the lives of previous generations, our leaders, and our founding fathers. By looking to our history, we can find hope, wisdom, and inspiration from those who fought for a better country in spite of the odds. We must re-learn the ways in which Americans have learned to survive—and thrive—despite unprecedented and seemingly insurmountable difficulties at home and abroad. No matter the challenge, Americans can respect each others' differences of opinion, honor diversity, and band together for change and a brighter future for those who will come after us.

America's future is in our hands.

BRIEF TIMELINE OF
AMERICAN HISTORY

1753   Liberty Bell is hung to commemorate the fifty year anniversary of Pennsylvania's original Constitution.

1770   Five civilians die at the hands of British soldiers during The Boston Massacre, sparking rebellion in some colonies.

1776   Declaration of Independence signed.

1783   Peace Treaty ends the Revolutionary War, with Britain surrendering all lands west of the Mississippi.

1787   Federal Convention held in Philadelphia to draft Constitution. Northwest Ordinance.

1788   Constitution ratified.

1789   Bill of Rights sent to states for ratification.

1791   Bill of Rights adopted as first ten amendments to the Constitution.

1793   Fugitive Slave Act.

1798	Alien and Sedition Act.
1803	Ohio admitted to United States. The Louisiana Purchase.
1804	Lewis and Clark expedition.
1808	Congress prohibits the importing of African slaves.
1809	James Madison elected President.
1812	War of 1812. Louisiana admitted to Union.
1814	Treaty of Ghent.
1816	Indiana admitted.
1817	Mississippi admitted. Erie Canal started.
1818	Treaty with Britain sets 49th Parallel.
1819	Treaty with Spain.
1820	Missouri Compromise.
1823	Monroe Doctrine.
1834	Indian Territory founded.
1836	Texas Revolution.
1838	Cherokee "Trail of Tears".

1840	Oregon Trail.
1845	1846 Mexican-American War (1846–1848).
1848	Gold discovered in California. Mexican Cession— end of Mexican War.
1850	Utah and New Mexico Territories.
1853	Gadsden Purchase.
1854	Nebraska and Kansas Territories.
1854	Republican Party formed for abolition of slavery.
1857	Dred Scott Decision. Kansas ratifies anti-slavery constitution.
1861	Civil War begins.
1863	Lincoln issues Emancipation Proclamation, freeing slaves.
1865	Lincoln assassinated. Reconstruction begins (1865–1877).
1865	Andrew Johnson elected President; Civil War ends.
1867	Alaska purchased. Midway annexed.
1883	Civil Service established.

1884	Alaska Territory organized.
1890	Oklahoma Territory organized. Sherman Antitrust Act. Massacre at Wounded Knee.
1896	Supreme Court rules "separate but equal" legal.
1898	Spanish-American War.
1901	President William McKinley shot by anarchist.
1902	Roosevelt begins conservation of forests.
1909	NAACP founded in New York City.
1913	World War I (1914–1918).
1917	Selective Service Act creates draft. U.S. declares war with Germany.
1920	Panama Canal completed. 18th Amendment prohibits alcohol. 19th Amendment gives women right to vote.
1924	Citizenship Act makes Native Americans citizens without impairing status as tribal members.
1929	Stock Market crashes.

1933	Roosevelt begins New Deal.
1935	Social Security Act provides retirement insurance.
1939	World War II begins.
1941	Japan surprise attack on Pearl Harbor. U.S. declares war with Japan.
1945	WWII ends.
1945	U.S. A-bombs Japan.
1947	Marshall Plan. Korean War (1950–53).
1955	Blacks boycott buses in Montgomery. Supreme Court orders school desegregation. AFL and CIO merge.
1961	Peace Corps.
1963	President John F. Kennedy assassinated.
1969	Apollo 11 mission. Neil Armstrong and Buzz Aldrin land on moon.
1970	U.S. invades Cambodia. EPA established.

1973	War Powers Act. Nixon resigns over Watergate. Endangered Species Act.
1975	Vietnam War ends.
1989	Gulf War (1990–1991).
1996	Welfare reform.
1999	National budget enters surplus.
2001	September 11th terror attack on the World Trade Center and the Pentagon. Patriot Act. No Child Left Behind.
2003	Iraq War begins.
2008	Barack Obama, first African-American President elected. Matthew Shepard and James Byrd Jr. Hate Crimes Prevention Act.
2010	Don't Ask, Don't Tell Repeal Act. Health Care and Education Reconciliation Act.

"America has believed that in differentiation, not in uniformity, lies the path of progress. It acted on this belief; it has advanced human happiness, and it has prospered."

—LOUIS D. BRANDEIS (1856–1941)
Supreme Court Justice

THE RIGHTS AND RESPONSIBILITIES OF AN AMERICAN CITIZEN

OF THE DEFINITIONS OF "CITIZEN" is: "a person that is a legally recognized as a member of a state, with associated rights and obligations." Just like any membership, belonging to the United States brings benefits as well as responsibilities.

As a member of the United States, every citizen holds rights granted to him or her by the Declaration of Independence and the Constitution. The government is bound to protect these rights, for everyone. However, it is the responsibility of Americans everywhere to be involved in our democracy and to protect the Constitution.

Following the list of rights of a citizen is a list of civilian responsibilities that apply to all Americans. Although these responsibilities are outlined in the Constitution, every American should strive to become an active participant in American civic life. Each one of us has an extraordinary opportunity to be a part of this great country.

YOUR RIGHTS

Freedom to express yourself. Freedom of expression includes the right to peaceably assemble in protest and the right to petition the government, as well as the right of every individual to express their thoughts, opinions, and feelings.

The right to express your beliefs is extremely precious, and it is protected by the Constitution. As an American, you have the right to think and say what you want about anything—including politics, the President, religion, music, art, entertainment, literature, the government, businesses, and more. Although we may not always all agree, the freedom of individuals to express what is on their minds ensures that this country will be rich with new ideas and opinions.

The freedom to speak out is powerful, and it also comes with responsibility. What you say cannot incite violence, endanger others, or obstruct anyone else's right to express himself or herself.

Freedom to worship as you wish. Freedom of religion is another of the most important rights of all Americans. The freedom to hold any religious belief, or none at all, is a fundamental right. Freedom of religion means that no one can force you to worship if you don't want to, or restrict how you want to worship, as long as your beliefs do not limit or endanger the religious practices of others.

There is no national religion in the United States. The government cannot tell you who or what or when to worship. Faith is personal and the government may not interfere with it.

Right to a prompt, fair trial by jury. Anyone who is accused of a crime has the right to a speedy and fair trial by a jury of their peers. Every individual is presumed innocent until proven guilty. A fair trial means that the accused has rights and that these rights must be respected. Some of these specific rights include: the accused has the right to legal representation in his own defense; the accused cannot be compelled to be a witness against him or herself; the accused must be informed of the nature of the charges brought against him or her; and many more. These rights ensure that everybody receives a fair trial, whether they are rich or poor, influential or infamous.

Right to keep and bear arms. The Bill of Rights addressed the right of individuals to "keep and bear arms" in its fourth Article; this became the second Amendment to the Constitution. The right to keep and bear arms means that every American has to right to maintain firearms for personal use and defense. This privilege can be reasonably restricted in the event that an individual intends to use firearms for a criminal purpose, or if the individual seems unfit to own a gun.

Right to vote in elections for public officials. The right of "one person, one vote" is an essential part of our democracy. Citizens choose their federal, state, and local leaders by voting. In this way,

Every citizen has the opportunity to express his or her political voice.

Right to apply for federal employment. Public service on behalf of, and in service to, the American people can be a very rewarding and fulfilling career. All U.S. citizens can apply for federal employment within a government agency or department.

Right to run for elected office. All American citizens, including naturalized citizens, have the right to run for elected office. However, Presidential and Vice Presidential candidates must be native-born citizens.

Freedom to pursue "life, liberty, and the pursuit of happiness." These three rights are defined by the Declaration of Independence as being "unalienable," meaning that they can never be given, taken away or surrendered. It is no surprise that our Founding Fathers chose to include "life" and "liberty" as basic freedoms, because of America's previous relations with Britain and their experiences with false imprisonment, unfair trials and cruel and unusual punishment.

Along with "life" and "liberty," American citizens are free to define and prsue his or her happiness as he or she sees fit. Like freedom of expression or freedom of religion, the freedom to create one's own "happiness" is the essence of American democracy. It is this freedom that sets America apart and has inspired immigrants, pioneers, inventors, entrepreneurs, teachers, artists, and many others. In short, the American citizen is free to follow his or her dreams.

"The future does not belong to those who are content with today, apathetic toward common problems and their fellow man alike, timid and fearful in the face of bold projects and new ideas. Rather, it will belong to those who can blend passion, reason and courage in a personal commitment to the ideals of American society. America's future is in our hands."

—ROBERT F. KENNEDY (1925–1968)
New York Senator and Champion of the Civil Rights Movement

YOUR RESPONSIBILITIES

To Support and defend the Constitution against all enemies, foreign and domestic. By taking the Oath of Office, an incoming President swears to "preserve, protect and defend the Constitution of the United States." In fact, this is also our duty. The first step to defending our freedom is to defend the Constitution and the rights it guarantees.

To Stay informed of the issues affecting your community. Becoming and involved citizen and staying informed about issues relevant to your local community, state, and federal government makes our democratic system even stronger.

Discussion, debate, a free and active press: these are even more ways to preserve our liberties and keep our republic healthy.

To Participate in the democratic process. Voting for local, state and federal office is an important way for everyone to stay involved in our community and our country. By voting, each individuals makes their opinions clear to elected officials. Your vote is your voice. Vote, register others to vote and fight to make sure every vote counts.

"I love America more than any other country in this world, and, exactly for this reason, I insist on the right to criticize her perpetually."

—JAMES BALDWIN (1924–1987)
Writer and Civil Rights Activist

To Respect and obey federal, state, and local laws. The rule of law was built into the Constitution—the Founding Fathers were explicit that laws may not be arbitrarily imposed or enforced, and there must be even-handedness in their prosecution.

Two hundred years later, the same rule applies. It is the responsibility of every American citizen to obey the laws of his locality, state and federal government. If he disagrees with the law, he must work to change it.

To Respect the rights, beliefs, and opinions of others. Just as we have the right to express ourselves as we see fit, we must respect the right of our fellow citizens to do the same. This can, at times, be difficult. Your neighbor may harbor views that are completely the opposite of yours. They may be views that enrage, disgust, or frighten you. But he or she has every right to hold them and express them, just as you are free to listen and argue or not. The democracy that debates within itself and adapts to changing values, is the democracy that flourishes.

To Participate in your local community. This is our country. It is up to us to keep a close watch on the actions of the men and women in Washington and step in when we disapprove, but we must also take action in our own communities and neighborhoods.

To Pay income and other taxes honestly, and on time, to federal, state, and local authorities. Our local, state, and federal governments must pay for the many services they provide us with, including road construction, education, the armed forces, and public assistance. These services are crucial. The American citizen pays his or her taxes on time and in full.

To Serve on a jury when called upon. The right to a "speedy and public trial by an impartial jury" is written into the Bill of Rights and the Constitution. To assure that every citizen gets a fair day in court, we must all serve as jurors when we are called upon to do so. It is another form of participation, another way our opinions and beliefs as individuals can help shape the society we live in.

To Defend the country if the need should arise. The Armed Forces of the United States is an all-volunteer force. However, other patriotic contributions, including civil service, are needed to defend this country—especially during wartime. When we set aside differences for the sake of our country, we are at our strongest. A citizen does not have to choose to be a member of the military to defend the United States and the ideals on which this country is founded.

II

The Documents
of
Democracy

"America is woven of many strands. I would recognize them and let it so remain. Our fate is to become one, and yet many. This is not prophecy, but description."

—RALPH ELLISON (1914–1994)
Scholar and Writer

THE DOCUMENTS IN THIS SECTION are tremendously powerful. They up-hold the rights and principles in our country's foundation, and it is these same rights and principles that shape our way of life to this very day.

Our Founding Fathers used the words in these documents to bring about great change. Their ideas launched a legacy of freedom and democracy, and created a government unlike any elsewhere in the world. America's history has in many ways been built on these documents and those individuals who had the courage to set their words out into the world in search of a better future. Today, the spirit of Independence and a commitment to freedom still rings true in American laws and in the lives of Americans.

"There is in this world no such force as the force of a person determined to rise. The human soul cannot be permanently chained."

—W.E.B. DU BOIS (1868–1963)
Co-Founder of the National Association for the Advancement of Colored People

THE DECLARATION OF INDEPENDENCE

INTRODUCTION

IN 1776, the delegates from twelve of the thirteen colonies met at the Second Continental Congress in Philadelphia to draft the Declaration of Independence and make known their intent to break free from English rule. It took almost a year before delegates appointed Thomas Jefferson (with help from others, including Benjamin Franklin and John Adams) to put pen to paper. The Declaration included a list of grievances, or complaints, regarding King George's rule. Among these were complaints about trade being cut off, arbitrary taxes being imposed, and the denial of the right to a trial by jury.

Jefferson sent the document to the full Continental Congress on July 2, 1776. The Declaration of Independence was adopted two days later, on July 4, 1776. A great democratic nation was born.

JOHN HANCOCK

(1737–1793)

―――――

*"The greatest ability in business
is to get along with others and
to influence their actions."*

―――――

John Hancock was President of the Second
Continental Congress and first Governor of
the Commonwealth of Massachusetts. A well-
known patriot of the American Revolution,
Hancock is best known for his memorable signature on the Declaration of Independence.

THE UNANIMOUS DECLARATION OF THE THIRTEEN UNITED STATES OF AMERICA

WHEN IN THE COURSE OF HUMAN EVENTS it becomes necessary for one people to dissolve the political bands which have connected them with another and to assume among the powers of the earth, the separate and equal station to which the Laws of Nature and of Nature's God entitle them, a decent respect to the opinions of mankind requires that they should declare the causes which impel them to the separation.

We hold these truths to be self-evident, that all men are created equal, that they are endowed by their Creator with certain unalienable Rights, that among these are Life, Liberty and the pursuit of Happiness.
—That to secure these rights, Governments are instituted among Men, deriving their just powers from the consent of the governed, —That whenever any Form of Government becomes destructive of these ends, it is the Right of the People to alter or to abolish it, and to institute new Government, laying its foundation on such principles and organizing

its powers in such form, as to them shall seem most likely to effect their Safety and Happiness. Prudence, indeed, will dictate that Governments long established should not be changed for light and transient causes; and accordingly all experience hath shewn that mankind are more disposed to suffer, while evils are sufferable than to right themselves by abolishing the forms to which they are accustomed. But when a long train of abuses and usurpations, pursuing invariably the same Object evinces a design to reduce them under absolute Despotism, it is their right, it is their duty, to throw off such Government, and to provide new Guards for their future security.

Such has been the patient sufferance of these Colonies; and such is now the necessity which constrains them to alter their former Systems of Government. The history of the present King of Great Britain is a history of repeated injuries and usurpations, all having in direct object the establishment of an absolute Tyranny over these States. To prove this, let Facts be submitted to a candid world.

He has refused his Assent to Laws, the most wholesome and necessary for the public good.

He has forbidden his Governors to pass Laws of immediate and pressing importance, unless suspended in their operation till his Assent should be obtained; and when so suspended, he has utterly neglected to attend to them.

He has refused to pass other Laws for the accommodation of large districts of people, unless those people would relinquish the right of Representation in the Legislature, a right inestimable to them and formidable to tyrants only.

He has called together legislative bodies at places unusual, uncomfortable, and distant from the depository of their Public Records, for the sole purpose of fatiguing them into compliance with his measures.

He has dissolved Representative Houses repeatedly, for opposing with manly firmness his invasions on the rights of the people.

He has refused for a long time, after such dissolutions, to cause others to be elected, whereby the Legislative Powers, incapable of Annihilation, have returned to the People at large for their exercise; the State remaining in the mean time exposed to all the dangers of invasion from without, and convulsions within.

He has endeavoured to prevent the population of these States; for that purpose obstructing the Laws for Naturalization of Foreigners; refusing to pass others to encourage their migrations hither, and raising the conditions of new Appropriations of Lands.

He has obstructed the Administration of Justice by refusing his Assent to Laws for establishing Judiciary Powers.

He has made Judges dependent on his Will alone for the tenure of their offices, and the amount an payment of their salaries.

He has erected a multitude of New Offices, and sent hither swarms of Officers to harass our people and eat out their substance.

He has kept among us, in times of peace, Standing Armies without the Consent of our legislatures.

He has affected to render the Military independent of and superior to the Civil Power.

He has combined with others to subject us to a jurisdiction foreign to our constitution, and unacknowledged by our laws; giving his Assent to their Acts of pretended Legislation: For quartering large bodies of armed troops among us:

For protecting them, by a mock Trial from

punishment for any Murders which they should commit on the Inhabitants of these States:

For cutting off our Trade with all parts of the world:

For imposing Taxes on us without our Consent:

For depriving us in many cases, of the benefit of Trial by Jury:

For transporting us beyond Seas to be tried for pretended offences:

For abolishing the free System of English Laws in a neighbouring Province, establishing therein an Arbitrary government, and enlarging its Boundaries so as to render it at once an example and fit instrument for introducing the same absolute rule into these Colonies

For taking away our Charters, abolishing our most valuable Laws and altering fundamentally the Forms of our Governments:

For suspending our own Legislatures, and declaring themselves invested with power to legislate for us in all cases whatsoever.

He has abdicated Government here, by declaring us out of his Protection and waging War against us.

He has plundered our seas, ravaged our Coasts burnt our towns, and destroyed the lives of our people.

He is at this time transporting large Armies of foreign Mercenaries to compleat the works of death, desolation, and tyranny, already begun with circumstances of Cruelty and Perfidy scarcely paralleled in the most barbarous ages, and totally unworthy the Head of a civilized nation.

He has constrained our fellow Citizens taken Captive on the high Seas to bear Arms against their Country, to become the executioners of their friends and Brethren, or to fall themselves by their Hands.

He has excited domestic insurrections amongst us, and has endeavoured to bring on the inhabitants of our frontiers, the merciless Indian Savages whose known rule of warfare, is an undistinguished destruction of all ages, sexes and conditions.

In every stage of these Oppressions We have Petitioned for Redress in the most humble terms: Our repeated Petitions have been answered only by repeated injury. A Prince, whose character is thus marked by every act which may define a Tyrant, is unfit to be the ruler of a free people.

Nor have We been wanting in attentions to our British brethren. We have warned them from time to time of attempts by their legislature to extend an unwarrantable jurisdiction over us. We have reminded them of the circumstances of our emigration and settlement here. We have appealed to their native justice and magnanimity, and we have conjured them by the ties of our common kindred. to disavow these usurpations, which would inevitably interrupt our connections and correspondence. They too have been deaf to the voice of justice and of consanguinity. We must, therefore, acquiesce in the necessity, which denounces our Separation, and hold them, as we hold the rest of mankind, Enemies in War, in Peace Friends.

We, therefore, the Representatives of the United States of America, in General Congress, Assembled, appealing to the Supreme Judge of the world for the rectitude of our intentions, do, in the Name, and by Authority of the good People of these Colonies, solemnly publish and declare, That these United Colonies are, and of Right ought to be Free and Independent States, that they are Absolved from all Allegiance to the British Crown, and that all political connection between them and the State of Great Britain, is and ought to be totally dissolved; and that as Free and Independent States, they have full Power to levy War, conclude Peace contract Alliances, establish Commerce, and to do all other Acts and Things which Independent States may of right do.

And for the support of this Declaration, with a firm reliance on the protection of Divine Providence, we mutually pledge to each other our Lives, our Fortunes and our sacred Honor.

— John Hancock
and the signers of the
Declaration of Independence

THE CONSTITUTION OF THE UNITED STATES

INTRODUCTION

THE FIRST ATTEMPT at a working Constitution was the Articles of Confederation, but after ten years, it became clear that the Articles would need to be revised. The Second Continental gathered at the State House in Philadelphia in 1787 and debated throughout the summer before the final draft of the Constitution was signed on September 17, 1787.

This unique document called for a central government with three branches, each restrained from exerting too much power via a system of checks and balances. It defined the roles each branch and also laid out a system of state's rights and granted states equal representation in the Senate, despite the state's size, with representation in the House to be determined by population.

ALEXANDER HAMILTON
(1755–1804)

———

"In framing a government which is to be administered by men over men the great difficulty lies in this: You must first enable the government to control the governed, and in the next place, oblige it to control itself."

———

Alexander Hamilton was one of our nation's Founding Fathers and the first U.S. Secretary of the Treasury. As a delegate to the Constitutional Convention, he also helped to write the Federalist Papers, which have become a primary source for interpretation of the Constitution.

THE CONSTITUTION OF THE UNITED STATES OF AMERICA

WE THE PEOPLE OF THE UNITED STATES, in order to form a more perfect union, establish justice, insure domestic tranquility, provide for the common defense, promote the general welfare, and secure the blessings of liberty to ourselves and our posterity, do ordain and establish this Constitution for the United States of America.

ARTICLE I — *The Legislative Branch*

Section 1 — The Legislature. All legislative powers herein granted shall be vested in a Congress of the United States, which shall consist of a Senate and House of Representatives.

Section 2 — The House. The House of Representatives shall be composed of members chosen every second year by the people of the several states, and the electors in each state shall have the qualifications requisite for electors of the most numerous branch of the state legislature.

No person shall be a Representative who shall not have attained to the age of twenty five years, and been seven years a citizen of the United States, and who shall not, when elected, be an inhabitant of that state in which he shall be chosen.

Representatives and direct taxes shall be apportioned among the several states which may be included within this union, according to their respective numbers, which shall be determined by adding to the whole number of free persons, including those bound to service for a term of years, and excluding Indians not taxed, three fifths of all other Persons. The actual Enumeration shall be made within three years after the first meeting of the Congress of the United States, and within every subsequent term of ten years, in such manner as they shall by law direct. The number of Representatives shall not exceed one for every thirty thousand, but each state shall have at least one Representative; and until such enumeration shall be made, the state of New Hampshire shall be entitled to chuse three, Massachusetts eight, Rhode Island and Providence Plantations one, Connecticut five, New York six, New Jersey four, Pennsylvania eight, Delaware one, Maryland six, Virginia ten, North Carolina five, South Carolina five, and Georgia three.

When vacancies happen in the Representation from any state, the executive authority thereof shall issue writs of election to fill such vacancies.

The House of Representatives shall choose their speaker and other officers; and shall have the sole power of impeachment.

Section 3 — The Senate. The Senate of the United States shall be composed of two Senators from each state, chosen by the legislature thereof, for six years; and each Senator shall have one vote.

Immediately after they shall be assembled in consequence of the first election, they shall be divided as equally as may be into three classes. The seats of the Senators of the first class shall be vacated at the expiration of the second year, of the second class at the expiration of the fourth year, and the third class at the expiration of the sixth year, so that one third may be chosen every second year; and if vacancies happen by resignation, or otherwise, during the recess of the legislature of any state, the executive thereof may make temporary appointments until the next meeting of the legislature, which shall then fill such vacancies.

No person shall be a Senator who shall not have attained to the age of thirty years, and been nine years a citizen of the United States and who shall not, when elected, be an inhabitant of that state for which he shall be chosen.

The Vice President of the United States shall be President of the Senate, but shall have no vote, unless they be equally divided. The Senate shall choose their other officers, and also a President pro tempore, in the absence of the Vice President, or when he shall exercise the office of President of the United States.

The Senate shall have the sole power to try all impeachments. When sitting for that purpose, they shall be on oath or affirmation. When the President of the United States is tried, the Chief Justice shall preside: And no person shall be convicted without the concurrence of two thirds of the members present.

Judgment in cases of impeachment shall not extend further than to removal from office, and disqualification to hold and enjoy any office of honor, trust or profit under the United States: but the party convicted shall nevertheless be liable and subject to indictment, trial, judgment and punishment, according to law.

Section 4 — Elections, Meetings. The times, places and manner of holding elections for Senators and Representatives, shall be prescribed in each state by the legislature thereof; but the Congress may at any time by law make or alter such regulations, except as to the places of choosing Senators.

The Congress shall assemble at least once in every year, and such meeting shall be on the first Monday in December, unless they shall by law appoint a different day.

Section 5—Membership, Rules, Journals, Adjournment. Each House shall be the judge of the elections, returns and qualifications of its own members, and a majority of each shall constitute a quorum to do business; but a smaller number may adjourn from day to day, and may be authorized to compel the attendance of absent members, in such manner, and under such penalties as each House may provide.

Each House may determine the rules of

its proceedings, punish its members for disorderly behavior, and, with the concurrence of two thirds, expel a member.

Each House shall keep a journal of its proceedings, and from time to time publish the same, excepting such parts as may in their judgment require secrecy; and the yeas and nays of the members of either House on any question shall, at the desire of one fifth of those present, be entered on the journal.

Neither House, during the session of Congress, shall, without the consent of the other, adjourn for more than three days, nor to any other place than that in which the two Houses shall be sitting.

Section 6 — Compensation. The Senators and Representatives shall receive a compensation for their services, to be ascertained by law, and paid out of the treasury of the United States. They shall in all cases, except treason, felony and breach of the peace, be privileged from arrest during their attendance at the session of their respective Houses, and in going to and returning from the same; and for any speech or debate in either House, they shall not be questioned in any other place.

No Senator or Representative shall, during the time for which he was elected, be appointed to any civil office under the authority of the United States, which shall have been created, or the emoluments whereof shall have been increased during such time: and no person holding any office under the United States, shall be a member of either House during his continuance in office.

Section 7 — Revenue Bills, Legislative Process, Presidential Veto. All bills for raising revenue shall originate in the House of Representatives; but the Senate may propose or concur with amendments as on other Bills.

Every bill which shall have passed the House of Representatives and the Senate, shall, before it become a law, be presented to the President of the United States; if he approve he shall sign it, but if not he shall return it, with his objections to that House in which it shall have originated, who shall enter the objections at large on their journal, and proceed to reconsider it. If after such reconsideration two thirds of that House shall agree to pass the bill, it shall be sent, together with the objections, to the other House, by

"Here in America we are descended in blood and in spirit from revolutionists and rebels—men and women who dare to dissent from accepted doctrine. As their heirs, may we never confuse honest dissent with disloyal subversion."

—DWIGHT D. EISENHOWER
(1890–1969)
Thirty-Fourth U.S. President

which it shall likewise be reconsidered, and if approved by two thirds of that House, it shall become a law. But in all such cases the votes of both Houses shall be determined by yeas and nays, and the names of the persons voting for and against the bill shall be entered on the journal of each House respectively. If any bill shall not be returned by the President within ten days (Sundays excepted) after it shall have been presented to him, the same shall be a law, in like manner as if he had signed it, unless the Congress by their adjournment prevent its return, in which case it shall not be a law.

Every order, resolution, or vote to which the concurrence of the Senate and House of Representatives may be necessary (except on a question of adjournment) shall be presented to the President of the United States; and before the same shall take effect, shall be approved by him, or being disapproved by him, shall be repassed by two thirds of the Senate and House of Representatives, according to the rules and limitations prescribed in the case of a bill.

Section 8 — Powers of Congress. The Congress shall have power to lay and collect taxes, duties, imposts and excises, to pay the debts and provide for the common defense and general welfare of the United States; but all duties, imposts and excises shall be uniform throughout the United States;

To borrow money on the credit of the United States;

To regulate commerce with foreign nations, and among the several states, and with the Indian tribes;

To establish a uniform rule of naturalization, and uniform laws on the subject of bankruptcies throughout the United States;

To coin money, regulate the value thereof, and of foreign coin, and fix the standard of weights and measures;

To provide for the punishment of counterfeiting the securities and current coin of the United States;

To establish post offices and post roads;

To promote the progress of science and useful arts, by securing for limited times to authors and inventors the exclusive right to their respective writings and discoveries;

To constitute tribunals inferior to the Supreme Court;

To define and punish piracies and felonies committed on the high seas, and offenses against the law of nations;

To declare war, grant letters of marque and reprisal, and make rules concerning captures on land and water;

To raise and support armies, but no appropriation of money to that use shall be for a longer term than two years;

To provide and maintain a navy;

To make rules for the government and regulation of the land and naval forces;

To provide for calling forth the militia to execute the laws of the union, suppress insurrections and repel invasions;

To provide for organizing, arming, and disciplining, the militia, and for governing such part of them as may be employed in the service of the United States, reserving to the states respectively, the appointment of the officers, and the authority of training the militia according to the discipline prescribed by Congress;

To exercise exclusive legislation in all cases whatsoever, over such District (not exceeding ten miles square) as may, by cession of particular states, and the acceptance of Congress, become the seat of the government of the United States, and to exercise like authority over all places purchased by the consent of the legislature of the state in which the same shall be, for the erection of forts, magazines, arsenals, dockyards, and other needful buildings; And

To make all laws which shall be necessary and proper for carrying into execution the foregoing powers, and all other powers vested by this Constitution in the government of the United States, or in any department or officer thereof.

Section 9 — Limits on Congress. The migration or importation of such persons as any of the states now existing shall think proper to admit, shall not be prohibited by the Congress prior to the year one thousand eight hundred and eight, but a tax or duty may be imposed on such importation, not exceeding ten dollars for each person.

The privilege of the writ of habeas corpus shall not be suspended, unless when in cases of rebellion or invasion the public safety may require it.

No bill of attainder or ex post facto Law shall be passed.

No capitation, or other direct, tax shall be

laid, unless in proportion to the census or enumeration herein before directed to be taken.

No tax or duty shall be laid on articles exported from any state.

No preference shall be given by any regulation of commerce or revenue to the ports of one state over those of another: nor shall vessels bound to, or from, one state, be obliged to enter, clear or pay duties in another.

No money shall be drawn from the treasury, but in consequence of appropriations made by law; and a regular statement and account of receipts and expenditures of all public money shall be published from time to time.

No title of nobility shall be granted by the United States: and no person holding any office of profit or trust under them, shall, without the consent of the Congress, accept of any present, emolument, office, or title, of any kind whatever, from any king, prince, or foreign state.

Section 10 — Powers Prohibited of States. No state shall enter into any treaty, alliance, or confederation; grant letters of marque and reprisal; coin money; emit bills of credit; make anything but gold and silver coin a tender in payment of debts; pass any bill of attainder, ex post facto law, or law impairing the obligation of contracts, or grant any title of nobility.

No state shall, without the consent of the Congress, lay any imposts or duties on imports or exports, except what may be absolutely necessary for executing it's inspection laws: and the net produce of all duties and imposts, laid by any state on imports or exports, shall be for the use of the treasury of the United States; and all such laws shall be subject to the revision and control of the Congress.

No state shall, without the consent of Congress, lay any duty of tonnage, keep troops, or ships of war in time of peace, enter into any agreement or compact with another state, or with a foreign power, or engage in war, unless actually invaded, or in such imminent danger as will not admit of delay.

ARTICLE II — *The Executive Branch*

Section 1 — The Executive Branch. The executive power shall be vested in a President of the United States of America. He shall hold his office during the term of four years, and, together with the Vice President, chosen for the same term, be elected, as follows:

Each state shall appoint, in such manner as the Legislature thereof may direct, a number of electors, equal to the whole number of Senators and Representatives to which the State may be entitled in the Congress: but no Senator or Representative, or person holding an office of trust or profit under the United States, shall be appointed an elector.

The electors shall meet in their respective states, and vote by ballot for two persons, of whom one at least shall not be an inhabitant of the same state with themselves. And they shall make a list of all the persons voted for, and of the number of votes for each; which list they shall sign and certify, and transmit sealed to the seat of the government of the United States, directed to the President of the Senate. The President of the Senate shall, in the presence of the Senate and House of Representatives, open all the certificates, and the votes shall then be counted. The person having the greatest number of votes shall be the President, if such number be a majority of the whole number of electors appointed; and if there be more than one who have such majority, and have an equal number of votes, then the House of Representatives shall

"Just what is it that America stands for? If she stands for one thing more than another it is for the sovereignty of self-governing people."

—WOODROW WILSON (1856–1924)
Twenty-eighth President

immediately choose by ballot one of them for President; and if no person have a majority, then from the five highest on the list the said House shall in like manner choose the President. But in choosing the President, the votes shall be taken by States, the representation from each state having one vote; A quorum for this purpose shall consist of a member or members from two thirds of the states, and a majority of all the states shall be necessary to a choice. In every case, after the choice of the President, the person having the greatest number of votes of the electors shall be the Vice President. But if there should remain two or more who have equal votes, the Senate shall choose from them by ballot the Vice President.

The Congress may determine the time of choosing the electors, and the day on which they shall give their votes; which day shall be the same throughout the United States.

No person except a natural born citizen, or a citizen of the United States, at the time of the adoption of this Constitution, shall be eligible to the office of President; neither shall any person be eligible to that office who shall not have attained to the age of thirty five years, and been fourteen Years a resident within the United States.

In case of the removal of the President from office, or of his death, resignation, or inability to discharge the powers and duties of the said office, the same shall devolve on the Vice President, and the Congress may by law provide for the case of removal, death, resignation or inability, both of the President and Vice President, declaring what officer shall then act as President, and such officer shall act accordingly, until the disability be removed, or a President shall be elected.

The President shall, at stated times, receive for his services, a compensation, which shall neither be increased nor diminished during the period for which he shall have been elected, and he shall not receive within that period any other emolument from the United States, or any of them.

Before he enter on the execution of his office, he shall take the following oath or affirmation:— "I do solemnly swear (or affirm) that I will faithfully execute the office of President of the United States, and will to the best of my ability, preserve, protect and defend the Constitution of the United States."

Section 2 — Civilian Power over Military, Cabinet, Pardon Power, Appoint-

ments. The President shall be commander in chief of the Army and Navy of the United States, and of the militia of the several states, when called into the actual service of the United States; he may require the opinion, in writing, of the principal officer in each of the executive departments, upon any subject relating to the duties of their respective offices, and he shall have power to grant reprieves and pardons for offenses against the United States, except in cases of impeachment.

He shall have power, by and with the advice and consent of the Senate, to make treaties, provided two thirds of the Senators present concur; and he shall nominate, and by and with the advice and consent of the Senate, shall appoint ambassadors, other public ministers and consuls, judges of the Supreme Court, and all other officers of the United States, whose appointments are not herein otherwise provided for, and which shall be established by law: but the Congress may by law vest the appointment of such inferior officers, as they think proper, in the President alone, in the courts of law, or in the heads of departments.

The President shall have power to fill up all vacancies that may happen during the

"There is in this world no such force as the force of a person determined to rise. The human soul cannot be permanently chained."

—W.E.B. DU BOIS (1868–1963)
Co-Founder of the National Association for the Advancement of Colored People

recess of the Senate, by granting commissions which shall expire at the end of their next session.

Section 3 — State of the Union, Convening Congress. He shall from time to time give to the Congress information of the state of the union, and recommend to their consideration such measures as he shall judge necessary and expedient; he may, on extraordinary occasions, convene both Houses, or either of them, and in case of disagreement between them, with respect to the time of adjournment, he may adjourn them to such time as he shall think proper; he shall receive ambassadors and other public ministers; he shall take care that the laws be faithfully executed, and shall commission all the officers of the United States.

Section 4 — Disqualification. The President, Vice President and all civil officers of the United States, shall be removed from office on impeachment for, and conviction of, treason, bribery, or other high crimes and misdemeanors.

ARTICLE **III** — *The Judicial Branch*

Section 1 — Judicial Powers. The judicial power of the United States, shall be vested in one Supreme Court, and in such inferior courts as the Congress may from time to time ordain and establish. The judges, both of the supreme and inferior courts, shall hold their offices during good behaviour, and shall, at stated times, receive for their services, a compensation, which shall not be diminished during their continuance in office.

Section 2 — Trial by Jury. The judicial power shall extend to all cases, in law and equity, arising under this Constitution, the laws of the United States, and treaties made, or which shall be made, under their authority; to all cases affecting ambassadors, other public ministers and consuls; to all cases of admiralty and maritime jurisdiction; to controversies to which the United States shall be a party; to controversies between two or more states; between a state and citizens of another state; between citizens of different states; between citizens of the same state claiming lands under grants of different states, and between a state, or the citizens thereof, and foreign states, citizens or subjects.

In all cases affecting ambassadors, other public ministers and consuls, and those in which a state shall be party, the Supreme Court shall have original jurisdiction. In all the other cases before mentioned, the Supreme Court shall have appellate jurisdiction, both as to law and fact, with such exceptions, and under such regulations as the Congress shall make.

The trial of all crimes, except in cases of impeachment, shall be by jury; and such trial shall be held in the state where the said crimes shall have been committed; but when not committed within any state, the trial shall be at such place or places as the Congress may by law have directed.

Section 3 — Treason. Treason against the United States, shall consist only in levying war against them, or in adhering to their enemies, giving them aid and comfort. No person shall be convicted of treason unless on the testimony of two witnesses to the same overt act, or on confession in open court.

The Congress shall have power to declare the punishment of treason, but no attainder of treason shall work corruption of blood, or forfeiture except during the life of the person attainted.

ARTICLE IV — *The States*
Section 1 — Each State to Honor all others. Full faith and credit shall be given

in each state to the public acts, records, and judicial proceedings of every other state. And the Congress may by general laws prescribe the manner in which such acts, records, and proceedings shall be proved, and the effect thereof.

Section 2 — State Citizens, Extradition. The citizens of each state shall be entitled to all privileges and immunities of citizens in the several states.

A person charged in any state with treason, felony, or other crime, who shall flee from justice, and be found in another state, shall on demand of the executive authority of the state from which he fled, be delivered up, to be removed to the state having jurisdiction of the crime.

No person held to service or labor in one state, under the laws thereof, escaping into another, shall, in consequence of any law or regulation therein, be discharged from such service or labor, but shall be delivered up on claim of the party to whom such service or labor may be due.

Section 3 — New States. New states may be admitted by the Congress into this union; but no new states shall be formed or erected within the jurisdiction of any other state; nor any state be formed by the junction of two or more states, or parts of states, without the consent of the legislatures of the states concerned as well as of the Congress.

The Congress shall have power to dispose of and make all needful rules and regulations respecting the territory or other property belonging to the United States; and nothing in this Constitution shall be so construed as to prejudice any claims of the United States, or of any particular state.

Section 4 — Republican Government. The United States shall guarantee to every state in this union a republican form of government, and shall protect each of them against invasion; and on application of the legislature, or of the executive (when the legislature cannot be convened) against domestic violence.

ARTICLE **V** — *Amendment*
The Congress, whenever two thirds of both houses shall deem it necessary, shall propose amendments to this Constitution, or, on the application of the legislatures of two thirds of the several states, shall call a convention for proposing amendments, which, in either case, shall be valid to all intents and purposes, as part of this Constitution, when ratified by the

legislatures of three fourths of the several states, or by conventions in three fourths thereof, as the one or the other mode of ratification may be proposed by the Congress; provided that no amendment which may be made prior to the year one thousand eight hundred and eight shall in any manner affect the first and fourth clauses in the ninth section of the first article; and that no state, without its consent, shall be deprived of its equal suffrage in the Senate.

ARTICLE VI — *Debts, Supremacy, Oaths*

All debts contracted and engagements entered into, before the adoption of this Constitution, shall be as valid against the United States under this Constitution, as under the Confederation.

This Constitution, and the laws of the United States which shall be made in pursuance thereof; and all treaties made, or which shall be made, under the authority of the United States, shall be the supreme law of the land; and the judges in every state shall be bound thereby, anything in the Constitution or laws of any State to the contrary notwithstanding.

The Senators and Representatives before

mentioned, and the members of the several state legislatures, and all executive and judicial officers, both of the United States and of the several states, shall be bound by oath or affirmation, to support this Constitution; but no religious test shall ever be required as a qualification to any office or public trust under the United States.

ARTICLE VII — *Ratification*

The ratification of the conventions of nine states, shall be sufficient for the establishment of this Constitution between the states so ratifying the same.

Done in convention by the unanimous consent of the states present the seventeenth day of September in the year of our Lord one . thousand seven hundred and eighty seven and of the independence of the United States of America the twelfth.

In witness whereof We have hereunto subscribed our Names,

— George Washington
*and the signers of the Constitution
of the United States of America*

THE BILL OF RIGHTS

INTRODUCTION

IN 1789, JAMES MADISON presented the First Congress of the United States with twelve proposed Amendments to the Constitution. These Amendments had been drafted to ensure the protection of individual freedoms against the government, protection that many felt was lacking from the Constitution. On December 15, 1791, ten of the twelve Amendments were ratified. These first ten Amendments to the Constitution are known as the Bill of Rights. The Bill of Rights guards the legal rights of American citizens, such as the right to a jury trial, the right to legal representation, protection from unreasonable searches and seizures, and freedom of religion.

The Bill of Rights is the crown jewel of our democracy. It defends the power of the individual against the power of government. Without the Bill of Rights, our freedoms could be threatened by changing popular opinion, prejudices or other pressures. But because of this document, those freedoms are secure. Today, the United States Supreme Court still hears cases concerning these most fundamental rights.

THOMAS JEFFERSON
(1743–1826)

―――――――

"A bill of rights is what the people are entitled to against every government on earth... and what no just government should refuse."

―――――――

One of the authors of the Declaration of Independence, Jefferson went on to become the Governor of Virginia and America's minister to France. He was elected the third President of the United States in 1800 and orchestrated the Louisiana Purchase.

The Bill of Rights

CONGRESS OF THE UNITED STATES begun and held at the City of New York, on Wednesday the fourth of March, one thousand seven hundred and eighty nine.

THE CONVENTIONS of a number of the States, having at the time of their adopting the Constitution, expressed a desire, in order to prevent misconstruction or abuse of its powers, that further declaratory and restrictive clauses should be added: And as extending the ground of public confidence in the Government, will best ensure the beneficent ends of its institution.

RESOLVED by the Senate and House of Representatives of the United States of America, in Congress assembled, two thirds of both Houses concurring, that the following Articles be proposed to the Legislatures of the several States, as amendments to the Constitution of the United States, all, or any of which Articles, when ratified by three fourths of the said Legislatures, to be valid to all intents and purposes, as part of the said Constitution; viz.

ARTICLES in addition to, and Amendment of the Constitution of the United States of America, proposed by Congress, and ratified by the Legislatures of the several States, pursuant to the fifth Article of the original Constitution.

ARTICLE THE FIRST... After the first enumeration required by the first article of the Constitution, there shall be one Representative for every thirty thousand, until the number shall amount to one hundred, after which the proportion shall be so regulated by Congress, that there shall be not less than one hundred Representatives, nor less than one Representative for every forty thousand persons, until the number of Representatives shall amount to two hundred; after which the proportion shall be so regulated by Congress, that there shall not be less than two hundred Representatives, nor more than one Representative for every fifty thousand persons.

ARTICLE THE SECOND... No law, varying the compensation for the services of the Senators and Representatives, shall take effect, until an election of Representatives shall have intervened.

ARTICLE THE THIRD... Congress shall make no law respecting an establishment of religion, or prohibiting the free exercise thereof; or abridging the freedom of speech, or of the press; or the right of the people peaceably to assemble, and to petition the Government for a redress of grievances.

ARTICLE THE FOURTH... A well regulated Militia, being necessary to the security of a free State, the right of the people to keep and bear Arms, shall not be infringed.

ARTICLE THE FIFTH... No Soldier shall, in time of peace be quartered in any house, without the consent of the Owner, nor in time of war, but in a manner to be prescribed by law.

ARTICLE THE SIXTH... The right of the people to be secure in their persons, houses, papers, and effects, against unreasonable searches and seizures, shall not be violated, and no Warrants shall issue, but upon probable cause, supported by Oath or affirmation, and particularly describing the place to be searched, and the persons or things to be seized.

ARTICLE THE SEVENTH... No person shall be held to answer for a capital, or otherwise infamous crime, unless on a presentment or indictment of a Grand Jury, except in cases arising in the land or naval forces, or in the

Militia, when in actual service in time of War or public danger; nor shall any person be subject for the same offence to be twice put in jeopardy of life or limb; nor shall be compelled in any criminal case to be a witness against himself, nor be deprived of life, liberty, or property, without due process of law; nor shall private property be taken for public use, without just compensation.

ARTICLE THE EIGHTH... In all criminal prosecutions, the accused shall enjoy the right to a speedy and public trial, by an impartial jury of the State and district wherein the crime shall have been committed, which district shall have been previously ascertained by law, and to be informed of the nature and cause of the accusation; to be confronted with the witnesses against him; to have compulsory process for obtaining witnesses in his favor, and to have the Assistance of Counsel for his defence.

ARTICLE THE NINTH... In Suits at common law, where the value in controversy shall exceed twenty dollars, the right of trial by jury shall be preserved, and no fact tried by a jury, shall be otherwise re-examined in any Court of the United States, than according to the rules of the common law.

ARTICLE THE TENTH... Excessive bail shall not be required, nor excessive fines imposed, nor cruel and unusual punishments inflicted.

ARTICLE THE ELEVENTH... The enumeration in the Constitution, of certain rights, shall not be construed to deny or disparage others retained by the people.

ARTICLE THE TWELFTH... The powers not delegated to the United States by the Constitution, nor prohibited by it to the States, are reserved to the States respectively, or to the people.

ATTEST,

—John Adams,
*and the signers
of the Bill of Rights*

THE EMANCIPATION PROCLAMATION

INTRODUCTION

ABRAHAM LINCOLN signed the Emancipation Proclamation on January 1, 1863. At the time, the Civil War had been raging for over two years. The Emancipation Proclamation freed slaves in the Northern, or Union, states. Many of those newly freed slaves joined the Union Army. In fact, by the war's end in 1865, almost 200,000 African-Americans had fought for the Union cause. The Emancipation Proclamation not only helped end a war that was dividing America, but also emphasized the importance of unity and freedom for all Americans, and, two years after the Emancipation Proclamation, the Thirteenth Amendment to the Constitution ended slavery in the United States.

In signing the Emancipation Proclamation, Abraham Lincoln led America one step closer toward realizing the vision of equality and individual liberty presented by the Declaration of Independence.

ABRAHAM LINCOLN
(1809–1865)

"As I would not be a slave, so I would not be a master. This expresses my idea of democracy."

Abraham Lincoln led our nation through the Civil War. Before becoming our nation's sixteenth President, he also worked as a lawyer, an Illinois state legislator, and was a member of the House of Representatives. He was later assassinated in 1865.

THE EMANCIPATION PROCLAMATION

By the

President of the United States of America:

A PROCLAMATION. Whereas, on the twenty-second day of September, in the year of our Lord one thousand eight hundred and sixty-two, a proclamation was issued by the President of the United States, containing, among other things, the following, to wit:

"That on the first day of January, in the year of our Lord one thousand eight hundred and sixty-three, all persons held as slaves within any State or designated part of a State, the people whereof shall then be in rebellion against the United States, shall be then, thenceforward, and forever free; and the Executive Government of the United States, including the military and naval authority thereof, will recognize and maintain the freedom of such persons, and will do no act or acts to repress such persons, or any of them, in any efforts they may make for their actual freedom.

"That the Executive will, on the first day of January aforesaid, by proclamation, designate the States and parts of States, if any, in which the people thereof, respectively, shall then be in rebellion against the United States; and the fact that any State, or the people thereof, shall on that day be, in good faith, represented in the Congress of the United States by members chosen thereto at elections wherein a majority of the qualified voters of such State shall have participated, shall, in the absence of strong countervailing testimony, be deemed conclusive evidence that such State, and the people thereof, are not then in rebellion against the United States."

Now, therefore I, Abraham Lincoln, President of the United States, by virtue of the power in me vested as Commander-in-Chief, of the Army and Navy of the United States in time of actual armed rebellion against the authority and government of the United States, and as a fit and necessary war measure for suppressing said rebellion, do, on this first day of January, in the year of our Lord one thousand eight hundred and sixty-three, and in accordance with my purpose so to do publicly proclaimed for the full period of one hundred days, from the day first above mentioned, order and designate as the States and parts of States wherein the people thereof respectively, are this day in rebellion against the United States, the following, to wit:

Arkansas, Texas, Louisiana, (except the Parishes of St. Bernard, Plaquemines, Jefferson, St. John, St. Charles, St. James Ascension, Assumption, Terrebonne, La-fourche, St. Mary, St. Martin, and Orleans, including the City of New Orleans) Mississippi, Alabama, Florida, Georgia, South Carolina, North Carolina, and Virginia, (except the forty-eight counties designated as West Virginia, and also the counties of Berkley, Accomac, Northampton, Elizabeth City, York, Princess Ann, and Norfolk, including the cities of Norfolk and Portsmouth[)], and which excepted parts, are for the present, left precisely as if this proclamation were not issued.

And by virtue of the power, and for the purpose aforesaid, I do order and declare that all persons held as slaves within said designated States, and parts of States, are, and henceforward shall be free; and that the Executive government of the United States, including the military and naval authorities thereof, will recognize and maintain the freedom of said persons.

And I hereby enjoin upon the people so declared to be free to abstain from all violence, unless in necessary self-defence; and I recommend to them that, in all cases when allowed, they labor faithfully for reasonable wages.

And I further declare and make known, that such persons of suitable condition, will be received into the armed service of the United States to garrison forts, positions, stations, and other places, and to man vessels of all sorts in said service.

And upon this act, sincerely believed to be an act of justice, warranted by the Constitution, upon military necessity, I invoke the considerate judgment of mankind, and the gracious favor of Almighty God.

In witness whereof, I have hereunto set my hand and caused the seal of the United States to be affixed.

Done at the City of Washington, this first day of January, in the year of our Lord one thousand eight hundred and sixty three, and of the Independence of the United States of America the eighty-seventh.

— Abraham Lincoln
President
William H. Seward
Secretary of State

III

By the People, for the People

"The cement of this union
is the heart-blood of every
American."

—THOMAS JEFFERSON (1743–1826)
Third U.S. President

As Americans, each one of us plays a role in shaping the future of our nation.

This opportunity to participate is our right and one that we should exercise with great pride and responsibility.

Our government was carefully structured by our founding fathers so that no one individual would have ultimate control. Instead, democracy and freedom for all is paramount. This ensures that the our government reflects the views and needs of the American people, and that it serves those needs in as many ways possible. This is why our founding fathers used the phrase "by the people, for the people" as a guiding principal for shaping our democracy.

As you look closely at the structure of American government, you will see how carefully each component works with another to guarantee that no single aspect of this structure can control the others. This system is meant to ensure that the voice of the people rings loudest in the halls of Washington and all across the country.

HOW THE UNITED STATES GOVERNMENT WORKS

FRANKLIN DELANO ROOSEVELT once said of the United States Constitution, "[It] has proven itself the most marvelously elastic compilation of rules of government ever written." As a blueprint for how the American government would operate, it is a remarkably farsighted document.

The delegates to the Constitutional Convention in 1787 were determined to construct a central government which was powerful, but not all-powerful. So they devised a system with three separate branches, the executive, the legislative, and the judicial, each with its own unique powers. By maintaining a balance of power, no one branch could ever become too mighty, and no one man, or small group, could gain control of the republic.

The United States government is made of three distinct branches: legislative, judicial, and executive. Each branch has its own unique powers. This structure ensures a balance of power so that no single group has complete control. At the same time, it maintains a strong central government.

Article I of the Constitution defines the powers of the legislative branch or Congress. The executive powers of the President are defined in Article 2. Judicial power, according to Article 3, rests with the Supreme Court and many lesser courts sprinkled throughout the country.

Three separate branches, each with the power to "check" the overreaching of the other two in order to protect the rights of citizens. For example, the President can veto bills approved by Congress; the President also nominates individuals to serve in the Federal judiciary, who Congress can reject. The Supreme Court can declare a law enacted by Congress or an action by the President unconstitutional. In turn, Congress can impeach the President and Federal court justices and judges. It's like an elaborate game of chess—each piece has its powers, and even a pawn can defeat the King.

THE EXECUTIVE BRANCH

The Executive Branch is made up of the President, Vice President, the Cabinet and their advisors. Together, they are responsible for enforcing the laws of the land.

- The President is the Leader of the country and Commander in Chief of the Military.

- The Vice President is President of the Senate. He or she becomes President if the President is unable to serve.

- The Cabinet is made up of the fifteen department heads. The Cabinet advises the President and helps devise policy and strategy.

- Independent Agencies are responsible for putting policy into action. Examples are the Central Intelligence Agency and Internal Revenue Service.

- Vice President: President of the Senate. Becomes President if the President is unable to serve.

- Departments: Department heads advise the President and help devise plans of action.

- Independent Agencies: Put policy into action or provide special services.

THE PRESIDENT

The President is the Head of the Executive Branch. He or she is also Head of State and Commander in Chief of the armed forces.

The Constitution defines the specific powers of the President. As Head of State, the President is responsible for meeting with ambassadors and other public ministers from foreign countries. The President also can make treaties with other countries and appoint ambassadors, but only with the Senate's approval.

As Commander in Chief, the President can authorize the use of troops overseas whether or not war is declared. However, to declare war, the President must have the approval of Congress.

The President is also responsible for selecting the heads of each Executive Branch or Cabinet department. These nominees must then be approved by the Senate.

Other Powers of the President:

- To give an annual State of the Union Address to Congress
- To recommend legislation to Congress
- To convene Congress on extraordinary occasions
- To adjourn Congress in special cases
- To "take care that the laws be faithfully executed"
- To fill in administrative vacancies during Congressional recesses
- To grant reprieves and pardons for offences against the U.S.

Requirements to be President. The President and the Vice President are the only officials elected by the entire country. What are the requirements to be President or Vice President?

- The candidate must be at least 35 years old
- The candidate must be a natural-born U.S. citizen and have lived in the U.S. for at least 14 years.

- When elected, the President serves a term of four years. At most, a President may serve two terms.

Impeachment. The President can be removed from office through the process of impeachment. The House of Representatives initiates the procedure. If the House of Representatives feel that the President has committed acts of "Treason, Bribery, or other High Crimes and Misdemeanors," they can impeach him with a majority vote.

Impeachment is similar to a legal indictment. It is important to note that it is not a conviction. Once the House votes for impeachment, the case goes to the Senate. Under the supervision of the Chief Justice of the Supreme Court, the Senate reviews the case and votes whether or not to convict the President; conviction requires a two-thirds majority. If convicted, the President is removed from office.

THE VICE PRESIDENT

The Vice President is the first in the line of Presidential succession. He or she will assume the Presidency if the President is unable to serve (due to the death, resignation, or illness).

The Vice President also acts as the presiding officer of the U.S. Senate. In this role, the Vice President can cast a vote in the event of a Senate deadlock. The Vice President also presides over and certifies the official vote count of the U.S. Electoral College.

The Vice President also sits on the President's Cabinet and takes on select diplomatic duites.

THE CABINET

The Cabinet is made up of the President's closest and most trusted advisors. It includes the Vice President and the heads (or "Secretaries") of the 15 executive departments, as well as the heads of certain independent agencies and other officials. It traditionally meets on a weekly basis.

The Cabinet Secretaries include: the Secretaries of Agriculture, Commerce, Defense, Education, Energy, Health and Human Services, Homeland Security, Housing and Urban Development, Interior, Labor, State, Transportation, Treasury, and Veterans Affairs, and the Attorney General.

PRESIDENTS OF THE UNITED STATES

PRESIDENT	TERM
1. George Washington	1789–1793
2. John Adams	1797–1801
3. Thomas Jefferson	1801–1805
4. James Madison	1809–1813
5. James Monroe	1817–1825
6. John Quincy Adams	1825–1829
7. Andrew Jackson	1829–1833
8. Martin Van Buren	1837–1841
9. William Henry Harrison	1841
10. John Tyler	1841–1845
11. James K. Polk	1845–1849
12. Zachary Taylor	1849–1850
13. Millard Fillmore	1850–1853
14. Franklin Pierce	1853–1857
15. James Buchanan	1857–1861
16. Abraham Lincoln	1861–1865
17. Andrew Johnson	1865–1869
18. Ulysses S. Grant	1869–1877
19. Rutherford B. Hayes	1877–1881
20. James Garfield	1881–1881
21. Chester A. Arthur	1881–1885
22. Grover Cleveland	1885–1889
23. Benjamin Harrison	1889–1893

PRESIDENT	TERM
24. Grover Cleveland	1893–1897
25. William McKinley	1897–1901
26. Theodore Roosevelt	1901–1905
27. William H. Taft	1909–1913
28. Woodrow Wilson	1913–1917
29. Warren G. Harding	1921–1923
30. Calvin Coolidge	1923–1925
31. Herbert C. Hoover	1929–1933
32. Franklin D. Roosevelt	1933–1945
33. Harry S. Truman	1945–1949
34. Dwight D. Eisenhower	1953–1961
35. John F. Kennedy	1961–1963
36. Lyndon B. Johnson	1963–1969
37. Richard M. Nixon	1969–1974
38. Gerald R. Ford	1974–1977
39. Jimmy Carter	1977–1981
40. Ronald W. Reagan	1981–1985
41. George H.W. Bush	1989–1993
42. William J. Clinton	1993–2001
43. George W. Bush	2001–2009
44. Barack H. Obama	2009–2017
45. Donald J. Trump	2017–

The Executive Departments

The executive departments serve a crucial role in developing and implementing the policies of the President. The Executive Departments include:

Secretary of State/Department of State. Established in 1789, the Department of State advises the President in the formulation and execution of foreign policy. The State Department negotiates treaties and agreements with foreign nations. It represents the United States at the United Nations and other international organizations, as well as at international conferences.

Department of the Treasury. The Department of the Treasury (established in 1789) formulates and advises on economic, financial, tax, and fiscal policies. It serves as the U.S. Government's financial agent and manufactures coins and currency. The Secretary serves as the Government's chief financial officer.

Secretary of Department of Defense. Organized in 1947, the Department of Defense is responsible for overseeing the Army, Navy, Marine Corps, and Air Force, as well as the members of the Reserve and National Guard and the Department's civilian employees.

Department of Justice. The Department of Justice (established 1870) enforces the law in the public interest. It prosecutes criminal and consumer cases, and enforces drug, immigration, and naturalization laws. The Attorney General can represent the Government before the U.S. Supreme Court in cases of exceptional importance.

Department of Education. Established in 1979, the Department of Education formulates policy relating to education. It oversees the many Federal assistance programs to states for education. The Secretary of Education advises the President on education plans, policies, and federal programs.

Department of Homeland Security. The most recent of the executive departments, the Department of Homeland Security was established in 2003. The Department's mission is to prevent terrorist attacks within the United States and reduce America's vulnerability to terrorism.

The Independent Agencies. Executive branch independent agencies are charged with serving the public interest and carrying out government operations. They range from domestic concerns to foreign policy ones, from the Ballistic Missile Defense Organization to the Bureau of Alcohol, Tobacco, & Firearms, from arms control to the Bureau of Engraving & Printing.

The heads of certain independent agencies have been given Cabinet-level rank and sits in on the cabinet's weekly meetings. These include the Administrator of the Environmental Protection Agency; the Director of the Office of Management and Budget; the Director of the National Drug Control Policy; the Assistant to the President for Homeland Security; and the U.S. Trade Representative.

THE LEGISLATIVE BRANCH

The Legislative Branch is the law-making branch of Government. The Congress is part of the legislative branch and is made up of two houses—the House of Representatives and the Senate. This two house system is known as a bicameral legislature.

Like the executive branch, Congress has its share of supporting agencies which are an official part of the legislative branch. These include the Government Printing Office (GPO), the Library of Congress (LC), and the Government Accountability Office (GAO).

THE US CONGRESS

It is the duty of Congress is to write, debate, and pass bills, which are then passed on to the President for approval. Other congressional duties include investigating issues of interest to the public and overseeing the executive and judicial branches.

The Powers of Congress. The Constitution grants Congress "all legislative powers." These include:

- Coining money
- Funding and maintaining military forces

- Framing U.S. foreign policy
- Declaring war on other countries
- Regulating interstate and foreign commerce
- Controlling federal taxing and spending
- Impeaching officials
- Amending the Constitution

The Constitution also includes a catchall phrase to define Congress's power—it has the authority to "make all laws which shall be necessary and proper." This ambiguous wording is sometimes called the Elastic Clause.

Congress's authority to investigate and oversee the executive branch and its departments and agencies is a crucial part of our system of checks and balances. Through Congressional oversight, Congress can summon senior officials to answer questions from members, order audits of agencies, and hold hearings to allow citizens to voice their grievances.

Congress also holds hearings in order to raise public awareness about select issues. Members of Congress may conduct these hearings to identify problems that require the drafting of new laws.

Electing Members of Congress. The entire House membership (435) faces re-election every two years. The Senate is a continuing body, with one-third of its members up for re-election every two years.

Numbering Congresses. Since the First Congress (1789–1791) all Congresses have been numbered in order.

THE HOUSE OF REPRESENTATIVES

There are a total of 435 members in the House of Representatives. Each member represents an area of his or her state, known as a congressional district. The number of representatives a state may seat is based on the number of districts in that state. The number of districts is determined by population; the U.S. Census Bureau's population count every ten years is essential to determining the number of districts a state requires.

Representatives are elected for two-year terms. They must be 25 years old, a citizen for at least seven years, and a resident of the state from which they are elected.

There are five additional members in the House—from Puerto Rico, Guam, American Samoa, the Virgin Islands, and the District of

"You gain strength, courage and confidence by every experience in which you really stop to look fear in the face. You are able to say to yourself, 'I have lived through this horror. I can take the next thing that comes along.' You must do the thing you think you cannot do."

—ELEANOR ROOSEVELT
(1884–1962)
*Journalist, Social Advocate,
and First Lady*

Columbia. While they may participate in the debates, they cannot vote.

The Powers of the House of Representatives. The House has two special functions. It can:

- Initiate laws to raise taxes
- Initiate impeachment hearings against a government official

THE SENATE

The Senate has 100 members. This even number can lead to voting deadlocks. As president of the Senate, the Vice President has the authority to cast the tie-breaking vote.

Senators are elected for six-year terms. They must be 30 years old, a citizen for at least nine years, and a resident of the state from which they are elected.

Powers of the Senate. According to the Constitution, the Senate can:

- Confirm or disapprove treaties
- Confirm or disapprove Presidential appointments, including executive department heads, Supreme Court justices, and ambassadors
- Hold an impeachment trial

HOW A BILL BECOMES A LAW

The process by which a proposed bill becomes a law is an impressive one. Before a bill gets to the President's desk, it

- Goes through a lengthy process.

- Must pass through Congress.

- Approval by Congress usually means a great deal of cooperation, compromise, and debate.

Submitting a Bill. A bill is a proposed law. Bills are usually proposed by individual members of Congress, but State legislatures can also submit potential bills to a member of Congress who is from their state. In this way, proposed bills can often be the direct expression of the needs or concerns of citizens. The President can also suggest a bill. However, a bill to raise taxes can only be initiated by the House of Representatives.

No matter how a bill is presented to a member of Congress, that member must then introduce the bill for general consideration. This is a relatively simple process. In the House, representatives drop a copy of the bill into a bin specifically dedicated to new bills.

In the Senate, a copy of the bill is given to the clerk at the President's desk.

A bill must pass both houses of Congress in order to become a law.

Committees. Before a bill can move on, it must be approved by committees. After a bill is introduced, it is assigned to a committee. This committee is "of primary jurisdiction," or one directly concerned with its content. Both the House and the Senate are divided into committees and sub-committees, each with their own special area of interest. (For example, there are over twenty House committees, divided into one hundred and four subcommittees.) These committees will hear hearings on a bill and vote to see if the bill should proceed further (usually, a hearing is heard by the subcommittee first before it is heard by the subcommittee). In order to determine their vote, witnesses may be called to testify as to why a bill is needed, and sub-committee members ask questions of the witnesses to determine the necessity of the bill. The voices and opinions of experts and regular citizens are crucial to life of any bill.

If the bill passes both the subcommittee and the committee, it is sent to the full House or Senate along with a Committee report, it goes on for consideration by the full committee. If the bill fails, it dies.

House Procedure. In the House, the committee-approved bill is read and time is allotted for debate. When the time for debate has expired, the bill is read a second time. At that point, members may offer amendments to the bill. These are debated and then voted on.

Finally, the House votes on the bill as it stands, or chooses to "recommit" the bill and send it back to committee. Representatives vote either verbally, or by using electronic voting cards, with an electronic tote board in the chamber recording totals.

If the House votes on the bill and it passes, legislation is approved and it is published.

Senate Procedure. Traditionally, Senate procedures are much looser than those in the House.

When a bill is being considered, each Senator has unlimited time to debate it (unless there has been a previous agreement establishing a time limit). During this time, amendments may be offered. In some cases, a Senator may offer an objection. A "filibuster" is when a Senator speaks about a bill for an extended period of time, never yielding the floor to another Senator. This tactic can delay a vote, stop action on a bill, or force a compromise. Debate is concluded when a Senator yields the floor and no one steps up to speak.

After all the Senators who wish to speak have, and all the bill's amendments have been considered, the bill is put forth for a vote.

The Senate often votes by a roll call; the Clerk calls out the name of the Senators in alphabetical order and they place their vote, which is then announced by the Clerk.

Conference. A bill that has been approved by the House and the Senate must be checked to assure that the versions are identical. Minor differences like punctuation are easy to fix. However, if there are major discrepancies between the two versions of a bill, a conference is called.

In a conference, members of both Houses work to resolve the differences between the two versions of the bill. Sometimes members agree quickly; other times, they propose a compromise that must then be voted on by both Houses. If there is no agreement, the bill can die.

The careful process of making sure a bill is exactly as it should be for both Houses may seem time consuming, but it is in fact part of

"If we did all the things we are capable of, we would literally astound ourselves."

—THOMAS EDISON (1847–1931)
*Inventor of the Phonograph
and Motion Picture Camera*

the system of "checks and balances" that is built into our government.

On to the President. After a proposed bill passes both houses of Congress by a majority vote, it is sent along to the President. Once the President signs the bill, it becomes law.

However, the President might not sign the bill. If he specifically rejects the bill (called a veto), the bill returns to Congress. It is voted on again, and if both houses of Congress pass the bill again, this time by a two-thirds majority, then the bill becomes law without the President's signature (this is called "overriding a veto"). If a two-thirds majority isn't achieved, the veto stands and the bill dies.

The President may also "sit" on the bill; that is, taking no action at all. If the President does not sign or veto the bill after ten business days, the bill becomes law without the President's signature. However, if Congress adjourns before the ten days are up, and the bill is still not signed by the President, the bill fails. This is known as a "pocket veto."

A Bill Becomes Law. If a bill has either been signed, its veto overridden, or ten days have passed without signature, it finally becomes a law. The Archivist of the United

States assigns it a number and publishes it in pamphlet form. Every law, public and private, is published in a document called the United States Statutes at Large.

The journey of a proposed bill may be long, but it is the length of its approval process that ensures that every law will be carefully debated and considered. Representatives, elected by American citizens, are there every step of the way, speaking and acting on behalf of the people. This guarantee that the intent and concerns of the American people is brought before the government is at the very core of our democracy.

THE JUDICIAL BRANCH

The Judicial Branch was established by Article III of the Constitution with the creation of the Supreme Court. This court is the highest court in the country (lower Federal courts were created by Congress, which decided they were necessary and established them using power granted from the Constitution).

Courts make decisions about the meaning of laws, how they are applied, and whether they violate the Constitution.

THE SUPREME COURT

Article III of the U.S. Constitution established the Supreme Court as the highest court in the United States.

One of the Supreme Court's most important responsibilities is to decide if a law or government action violates the Constitution. This process is called judicial review. The Supreme Court can invalidate both federal and state laws if they conflict with the Constitution. Since the Supreme Court stands as the ultimate authority in constitutional interpretation, its decisions can be changed only by another Supreme Court decision or by a constitutional amendment.

Judicial review also puts the Supreme Court in a pivotal role in the American political system by making it the referee in disputes among various branches of the Federal and state governments.

The Supreme Court exercises complete authority over the federal courts, but it has only limited power over state courts because it cannot interpret state laws or issues arising under state constitutions, and it does not supervise state court operations. The Supreme Court makes the final decision on cases heard by federal courts, and it writes procedures that these courts must follow. All federal and state courts must abide by the Supreme Court's interpretation of federal laws and the Constitution of the United States.

Cases Brought Before the Court. When a case comes to the Supreme Court, several things happen. First, the Justices meet to decide if a case really involves Constitutional or federal law. This is done because a Supreme Court ruling can affect the outcome of hundreds or even thousands of cases in lower courts around the country, so it is important that the Court tries to use this enormous power only when a case presents a pressing constitutional issue.

Once the Justices decide to take a case, the lawyers for each side have one-half hour in which to present their side of the case in what is called "oral argument." The Justices can interrupt to ask questions at any time.

It takes a majority of Justices to decide a case. If the Chief Justice sides with the majority, he will write the majority opinion or assign it to one of the other Justices on the majority side to write. If the Chief Justice is not in the majority, the most senior Justice (the one who has served on the court the longest) will write the opinion or assign it to another Justice. These opinions must be carefully worded because they become the basis upon which similar cases will be argued in the future.

LANDMARK DECISIONS
OF THE U.S. SUPREME COURT

Since it first convened in 1790, the U.S. Supreme Court has been the central arena for debate on some of America's most important social and public policy issues including civil rights, powers of government, and equal opportunity. As the ultimate authority on constitutional law, the Supreme Court attempts to settle disputes when it appears that federal, state, or local laws conflict with the Constitution. The Supreme Court's decisions determine how America's principles and ideals, as expressed in the Constitution, are carried out in everyday life. These decisions impact the lives of all Americans. In the following section, you will read about several landmark decisions of the Supreme Court that are important to know and understand as a United States citizen.

Marbury v. Madison. While the U.S. Supreme Court wields immense power in determining the constitutionality of federal laws, its authority was still uncertain until 1803. Although most of the framers expected the Supreme Court to perform this essential role, the Court's authority was not explicitly defined in the Constitution. Chief Justice John Marshall's decision in Marbury v. Madison established the power of judicial review, making the Supreme Court an equal partner in government along with the Legislative and Executive branches. The Supreme Court now serves as the final authority on the Constitution.

The Marbury case began in 1801, during the last few weeks of President John Adams's term as President, and just before Thomas Jefferson became President.

Shortly before leaving office, President Adams had approved the appointment of several new justices of the peace including the appointment of William Marbury. However, Adams' Secretary of State, John Marshall, did not deliver commissions to all those appointed, thus prompting Thomas Jefferson, upon taking office, to order *his* Secretary of State James

Madison to withhold Marbury's appointment. Without Jefferson's approval, Marbury was unable to assume his positions as justice of the peace, and immediately turned to the Supreme Court in hopes that James Madison could be forced to acknowledge the appointment. So, Marshall made the crucial decision that the refusal of Marbury's appointment was indeed in violation of his rights as defined by the Constitution, and most importantly, that the Supreme Court held the responsibility of determining what is constitutional and what is not.

Excerpt: John Marshall Delivering the Opinion of the Court

"...The question, whether an act, repugnant to the constitution, can become the law of the land, is a question deeply interesting to the United States; ... That the people have an original right to establish, for their future government, such principles as, in their opinion, shall most conduce to their own happiness, is the basis on which the whole American fabric has been erected....

"Certainly all those who have framed written constitutions contemplate them as forming the fundamental and paramount law of the nation, and consequently, the theory of every such government must be, that an act of the legislature, repugnant to the constitution, is void.

"This theory is essentially attached to a written constitution, and is, consequently, to be considered, by this court, as one of the fundamental principles of our society."

Plessy v. Ferguson. While great strides were made in establishing the political rights of African Americans following the American Civil War, the U.S. Supreme Court delivered several decisions, most notably in the case of Plessy v. Ferguson, that impeded civil rights efforts in the United States.

Beginning in 1887, states began to require that railroads furnish separate accommodations for each race.

On June 7, 1892, Homer Plessy, an African American from New Orleans, boarded a train and sat in a rail car for white passengers. A conductor asked him to move, but Plessy refused, and was then arrested. Plessy challenged his arrest in court and argued that segregation violated both the Thirteenth and Fourteenth Amendments to the U.S. Constitution. Through appeal, the case was heard before the U.S. Supreme Court in 1896. By an eight to one decision, the Court ruled against Plessy, thus establishing the "separate but equal" rule, which mandated separate accommodations for blacks and whites on buses, trains, and in hotels, theaters, and schools.

In a powerful dissent, Justice John Marshall Harlan disagreed with the majority, stating "Our Constitution is color-blind, and neither knows nor tolerates classes among citizens." Harlan's words provided inspiration to many involved in the civil rights movement, including Thurgood Marshall, whose arguments in Brown v. Board of Education helped overturn the "separate but equal" precedent in 1954.

Excerpt: John Marshall Harlan Delivering the Dissenting Opinion of the Court

"In respect of civil rights, common to all citizens, the Constitution of the United States does not, I think permit any public authority to know the race of those entitled to be protected in the enjoyment of such rights.... [I]n the view of the Constitution, in the eye of the law, there is in this country no superior, dominant, ruling class of citizens. There is no caste here. Our Constitution is color-blind and neither knows nor tolerates classes among citizens. In respect of civil rights, all citizens are equal before the law. The humblest is the peer of the most powerful. The law regards man as man and takes no account of his surroundings or of his color when his civil rights as guaranteed by the supreme law of the land are involved...."

West Virginia State Board of Education v. Barnette. In 1940, as most of Europe was at war with Nazi Germany and the United States was increasing in support of Great Britain, a wave of patriotism swept the country. During this time, the U.S. Supreme Court ruled that public school students were required to salute the American flag and recite the Pledge of Allegiance, regardless of personal religious beliefs. Despite the ruling, many students resisted saluting the flag and reciting the Pledge of Allegiance due to their religious beliefs, and were consequently persecuted for their beliefs.

In 1943, the Court heard arguments in the case of West Virginia State Board of Education v. Barnette. This case concerned a requirement that all teachers and students must salute the flag as part of their daily program. Refusal to do so resulted in harsh punishment, including, in some cases, expulsion. After reviewing arguments on both sides, the Court ruled that this required activity violated the First Amendment.

Excerpt: Robert Jackson Delivering the Opinion of the Court

"...The very purpose of a Bill of Rights was to withdraw certain subjects from the vicissitudes of political controversy, to place them beyond the reach of majorities and officials and to establish them as legal principles to be applied by the courts. One's right to life, liberty, and property, to free speech, a free press, freedom of worship and assembly, and other fundamental rights may not be submitted to vote; they depend on the outcome of no elections....

"If there is any fixed star in our constitutional constellation, it is that no official, high or petty, can prescribe what shall be orthodox in politics, nationalism, religion, or other matters of opinion or force citizens to confess by word or act their faith therein. If there are any circumstances which permit an exception, they do not now occur to us...."

Brown v. Board of Education. Since the U.S. Supreme Court's 1896 decision in the case of Plessy v. Ferguson, racially segregated public schools were accepted under the basis of the "separate but equal" rule. Many civil rights groups, including the National Association for the Advancement of Colored People (NAACP), worked to overturn this ruling for several decades. In 1953, the NAACP brought five cases before the Supreme Court that directly challenged the precedent established in Plessy v. Ferguson.

These cases illustrated that many public schools in America were not providing equal facilities and materials to African American students. Thurgood Marshall, the NAACP's lead attorney, argued that the "separate but equal" rule violated the Fourteenth Amendment to the Constitution, which granted citizenship and equal protection to all citizens regardless of color.

On May 17, 1954, the segregation of public schools was in fact a violation of the Fourteenth Amendment and was therefore unconstitutional. This historic decision ended the "separate but equal" rule that had been in place for nearly six decades. Furthermore, the Court's decision in this landmark case helped expand the civil rights movement in the United States by advancing the idea that every American citizen deserves the promise of equality and justice under the law.

Excerpt: Earl Warren Delivering the Opinion of the Court

"...We come then to the question presented: Does segregation of children in public schools solely on the basis of race, even though the physical facilities and other "tangible" factors may be equal, deprive the children of the minority group of equal educational opportunities? We believe that it does....To separate them from others of similar age and qualifications solely because of their race generates a feeling of inferiority as to their status in the community that may affect their heart and minds in a way unlikely ever to be undone....

We conclude that in the field of public education the doctrine of "separate but equal" has no place. Separate educational facilities are inherently unequal...."

142

STATES RIGHTS
FEDERAL VERSUS STATE GOVERNMENT

IN THE UNITED STATES, power is shared between the national government and the state governments. The Constitution is very specific about the roles and powers of the central and state governments, and defines and limits the power of the national government as well as the relationship between the national government and individual state governments. Above all, this system, which allows for unity as well as diversity, is designed to protect the rights and freedoms of American citizens.

This balanced system took time to develop. The United States began as a federation of independent colonies, banding together against a repressive central government in Britain. For the first 100 years of America's history, most of the laws and policies that affected the people were created and enforced by individual states. The national government focused mostly on foreign affairs. However, following the great conflict of the Civil War, the importance of a central government that would set social and economic policy became clear. At this time, the 13th, 14th, and 15th Constitutional Amendments were passed. Following the Great Depression, when it became clear that states alone could not handle economic crises, Roosevelt's "New Deal" clarified the responsibilities of the federal government while also encouraging national, state and local governments to work together regarding specific issues.

Today, the federal government is the source of many of the funds states require to maintain roads, schools, and social programs. But states may pass laws concerning certain policies, such as the death penalty, marriage, and contraception, which are outside the bounds of federal control. This allows each state to make decisions and adopt laws based on their unique needs, history and philosophy.

State Government. Every state government has its own constitution, but it cannot conflict with terms of the national Constitution. Each state's constitution is different from another.

In general, state governments have the right to:

- Issue licenses

- Regulate businesses within the state

- Conduct elections

- Establish local governments

- Ratify amendments to the Constitution
- Take measures for public health and safety
- Exert any powers the Constitution does not delegate to the national government or prohibit the states from using (The Elastic Clause)

FEDERAL GOVERNMENT

The federal government is granted the power to:

- Print money
- Regulate interstate (between states) and international trade
- Make treaties and conduct foreign policy
- Declare war
- Provide an army and navy
- Establish post offices
- Make laws necessary and proper to carry out the these powers

The federal and state governments also share certain powers. These are called concurrent powers. These include the power to:

- Collect taxes
- Build roads
- Borrow money
- Establish courts
- Make and enforce laws
- Charter banks and corporations
- Spend money for the general welfare
- Take private property for public purposes, with just compensation

What the Federal and State Governments Can't Do. The Constitution and its amendments outline the many functions and powers of government. They also contain some prohibitions. In other words, things government cannot do.

The federal and state governments may not:

- Grant titles of nobility
- Permit slavery (13th Amendment)
- Deny citizens the right to vote because of race, color, or previous servitude (15th Amendment)
- Deny citizens the right to vote because of gender (19th Amendment)

STATES AND THEIR CAPITALS

State	Capital	Date of Statehood
Alabama	Montgomery	1819
Alaska	Juneau	1959
Arizona	Phoenix	1912
Arkansas	Little Rock	1836
California	Sacramento	1850
Colorado	Denver	1876
Connecticut	Hartford	1788
Delaware	Dover	1787
Florida	Tallahassee	1845
Georgia	Atlanta	1788
Hawaii	Honolulu	1959
Idaho	Boise	1890
Illinois	Springfield	1818
Indiana	Indianapolis	1816
Iowa	Des Moines	1846
Kansas	Topeka	1861
Kentucky	Frankfort	1792
Louisiana	Baton Rouge	1812
Maine	Augusta	1820
Maryland	Annapolis	1788
Massachusetts	Boston	1788
Michigan	Lansing	1837
Minnesota	Saint Paul	1858
Mississippi	Jackson	1817
Missouri	Jefferson City	1821

STATES AND THEIR CAPITALS

State	Capital	Date of Statehood
Montana	Helena	1889
Nebraska	Lincoln	1867
Nevada	Carson City	1864
New Hampshire	Concord	1788
New Jersey	Trenton	1787
New Mexico	Santa Fe	1912
New York	Albany	1788
North Carolina	Raleigh	1789
North Dakota	Bismarck	1889
Ohio	Columbus	1803
Oklahoma	Oklahoma City	1907
Oregon	Salem	1859
Pennsylvania	Harrisburg	1787
Rhode Island	Providence	1790
South Carolina	Columbia	1788
South Dakota	Pierre	1889
Tennessee	Nashville	1796
Texas	Austin	1845
Utah	Salt Lake City	1896
Vermont	Montpelier	1791
Virginia	Richmond	1788
Washington	Olympia	1889
West Virginia	Charleston	1863
Wisconsin	Madison	1848
Wyoming	Cheyenne	1890

NATIONAL SECURITY
AND DEFENSE

ARTICLE TWO, SECTION TWO of the United States Constitution lays out the President's responsibilities as Commander in Chief of the Armed Forces. "The President shall be Commander in Chief of the Army and Navy of the United States and of the Militia of the several States, when called into the actual Service of the United States," it reads. "[H]e may require the Opinion, in writing, of the principal Officer in each of the executive Departments, upon any Subject relating to the Duties of their respective Offices."

Over two hundred years later, this basic structure remains in place. The President, advised by the Secretary of Defense and the Chairman of the Joint Chiefs of Staff, has sole decision-making powers when it comes to issues of military force. He is the senior military authority in the nation, responsible for the protection of the United States from all enemies, foreign and domestic. It has been, and remains, an awesome responsibility.

Since the early days of the Republic, the

size and composition of America's national security apparatus have changed markedly. The Secretary of Defense, as the head of the Department of Defense, is the umbrella beneath which a massive organization goes about its duties. The Department of Defense maintains more than 5,000 different locations or sites domestically, totaling over 30 million acres of land. It has an annual budget of over $400 billion and almost a million civilian employees. As an entity, the Department of Defense rivals the world's biggest multi-national corporations for personnel and budget. America's military presence is now felt worldwide, in more than 163 countries.

The role of the American military has changed, as well. Fighting wars is now supplemented with providing humanitarian aid and disaster relief to foreign countries devastated by natural and man-made calamities, as well as peacekeeping functions. Since the September 11, 2001 terrorist attacks, the armed forces are also charged with Homeland Security, defending the territory of the United States against all forms of aggression, including terrorism.

Structure. Together, the President and his Secretary of Defense make up the Nation-

"I may be compelled to face danger, but never fear it, and while our soldiers can stand and fight, I can stand and feed and nurse them."

—CLARA BARTON (1821–1912)
Founder of the American Red Cross

al Command Authority. Their directives are communicated through the Office of the Secretary of defense to the military departments, the Chairman of the Joint Chiefs of Staff, and the unified commands.

MILITARY DEPARTMENTS

The military departments train and equip the military forces. The three main military departments are the Army, Navy and Air Force; the Marines are part of the Department of the Navy.

Army. The Army defends the land mass of the United States, its territories, commonwealths, and possessions. Its mission is to protect the Nation from its enemies, defend its vital national interests and provide support to civil authorities in response to domestic emergencies.

Navy. The Navy maintains, trains, and equips combat-ready maritime forces. Its goals are to maintain a worldwide presence, credible deterrence and dissuasion, projection of power from naval platforms anywhere on the globe, and the ability to prevail at sea.

Air Force. The Air Force is charged with providing the Nation with a powerful deterrent force in times of peace, and it sets the conditions for Joint and Coalition victory in times of war. It is capable of delivering forces anywhere in the world in less than forty-eight hours.

Marine Corps. The U.S. Marine Corps is responsible for providing power projection from the sea, utilizing the mobility of the U.S. Navy to rapidly deliver combined-arms task forces to global crises and hot spots.

Homeland Security. The Department of Homeland Security was established in the aftermath of the 9/11 attacks in order to better coordinate the activities of the domestic wing of the armed forces. These include the Coast Guard and the National Guard and Reserve.

Coast Guard The U.S. Coast Guard provides law and maritime safety enforcement, marine and environmental protection, and military naval support. They patrol our shores, perform emergency rescue operations, contain and clean up oil spills, and interdict drug and contraband smuggling.

National Guard & Reserve. The National Guard and Reserve forces provide wartime military support. They are essential to humanitarian and peacekeeping operations.

WAR AND MILITARY ACTION TIMELINE

1637 Pequot War between alliance of Massachusetts Bay and Plymouth colonies with Native American allies

1770 Five civilians die at the hands of British soldiers during The Boston Massacre, sparking rebellion in some colonies

1783 Peace Treaty ends the Revolutionary War, with Britain surrendering all lands west of the Mississippi

1786 Shay's Rebellion erupts in response to high taxes and penalties placed on farmers

1812 War of 1812 over Britain's interference in American maritime shipping and westward expansion

1814 Treaty of Ghent ends War of 1812

1818 Treaty with Britain sets 49th Parallel

1819 Treaty with Spain declares Florida as American territory

1823 Monroe Doctrine prohibits Britain from interfering in all American affairs

WAR AND MILITARY ACTION TIMELINE

continued

1836 Texas becomes independent from Mexico during the Texas Revolution

1846 Mexican War to gain southwest territory

1848 Treaty of Guadalupe Hidalgo ends Mexican War

1861 Civil War begins over the expansion of slavery

1863 Lincoln issues Emancipation Proclamation to free slaves in the Confederate states

1865 Civil War ends

1876 Sioux Indians, led by Sitting Bull, defeat Lt. Col. George A. Custer during the Battle of Little Bighorn

1883 Civil Service established

1890 Battle at Wounded Knee Creek is the last major conflict of the Indian Wars

1898 Spanish-American War. Treaty of Paris

1901 President McKinley shot by anarchist

1914 World War I begins. U.S. declares war on Germany

1917 Selective Service Act creates draft. U.S. declares war with Austria-Hungary

1918 Treaty signed to end World War I

1921 President Harding declares peace with Austria and Germany

1941 Japan surprise attack on Pearl Harbor. U.S. enters World War II against Japan, Germany, and Italy

1945 Germany surrenders. U.S. drops atomic bombs in Hiroshima and Nagasaki, Japan. Japan surrenders and World War II ends. United Nations is established

1947 Marshall Plan passed for post-war aid in Europe

1949 NATO is established

1950 U.S. enters Korean War in response to Communist forces

1953 Armistice agreement signed to end the Korean War

1959 Vietnam War begins in opposition to Communist forces in North Vietnam

WAR AND MILITARY ACTION TIMELINE

continued

1963 Kennedy assassinated

1970 U.S. invades Cambodia

1973 U.S. troops leave Vietnam. War Powers Act prohibits U.S. President from entering into military action without approval of Congress

1990 U.S. enters into the Gulf War

1991 Iraq accepts UN ceasefire to end the Gulf War

1998 U.S. attacks Sudan and Afghanistan in response to terrorist attacks on U.S. embassies in Kenya and Tanzania

2001 September 11th terror attack on the World Trade Center and the Pentagon, U.S. enters into the Afghanistan War

2003 Iraq War begins

2007 Iraq War De-Escalation Act

2008 US-Iraq Status of Forces Agreement

2011 American troops withdraw from Iraq

IV

The Voices
of Freedom

"The minute a person whose word means a great deal to others dare to take the open-hearted and courageous way, many others follow."

—MARIAN ANDERSON (1902–1993)
African-American singer, performer, and recipient of the UN Peace Prize and the Eleanor Roosevelt Human Rights Award

EVERY AMERICAN IS GRANTED freedom of expression, a right guarded by the third article of the Bill of Rights. It is this right that guarantees every American the right to raise their voices and speak their mind. Throughout America's history, many great Americans have used the power of words—whether spoken in celebration, or in protest, during trying times or moments of victory—to direct some of our country's greatest milestones.

On the following pages, you will find words of Presidents, dedicated activists, and speakers who inspired action and paved the way towards a brighter future for all Americans.

From the patriotic speeches of Presidents, including George Washington and John F. Kennedy, to the call for change voiced by activists like Sojourner Truth and Elizabeth Cady Stanton, these words express an unwavering commitment to the American dream for all Americans.

GEORGE WASHINGTON
(1732–1799)

"The basis of our political systems is the
right of the people to make and to alter their
constitutions of government"

George Washington was the first President
of the United States. He served as commander-
in-chief of the Continental Army in the Revolutionary War and later helped in drafting the
United States Constitution.

GEORGE WASHINGTON'S

FAREWELL ADDRESS

As the Commander in Chief of the Continental Army during the Revolutionary War, George Washington helped guide our country to freedom against the British Redcoats and later became the nation's first leader when he was unanimously elected as President in 1789. In the following speech, his farewell address after serving as President for two terms, Washington expresses a sense of hope and pride for his country—the sentiments on which American patriotism has been born.

SEPTEMBER 17, 1796

The period for a new election of a citizen, to administer the executive government of the United States, being not far distant, and the time actually arrived, when your thoughts must be employed designating the person, who is to be clothed with that important trust, it appears to me proper, especially as it may conduce to a more distinct expression of the public voice, that I should now apprize you of the resolution I have formed, to decline being considered among the number of those out of whom a choice is to be made.

I beg you at the same time to do me the justice to be assured that this resolution has not been taken without a strict regard to all the considerations appertaining to the relation which binds a dutiful citizen to his country; and that in withdrawing the tender of service, which silence in my situation might imply, I am influenced by no diminution of zeal for your future interest, no deficiency of grateful respect for your past kindness, but am supported by a full conviction that the step is compatible with both.

The acceptance of, and continuance hitherto in, the office to which your suffrages have twice called me, have been a uniform sacrifice of inclination to the opinion of duty, and to a deference for what appeared to be your desire. I constantly hoped, that it would have been much earlier in my power, consistently with motives, which I was not at liberty to disregard, to return to that retirement, from which I had been reluctantly drawn. The strength of my inclination to do this, previous to the last election, had even led to the preparation of an address to declare it to you; but mature reflection on the then perplexed and critical posture of our affairs with foreign nations, and the unanimous advice of persons entitled to my confidence impelled me to abandon the idea.

I rejoice, that the state of your concerns, external as well as internal, no longer renders the pursuit of inclination incompatible with the sentiment of duty, or propriety; and am persuaded, whatever partiality may be retained for my services, that, in the present circumstances of our country, you will not disapprove my determination to retire.

The impressions, with which I first undertook the arduous trust, were explained on the proper occasion. In the discharge of this trust, I will only say, that I have, with good intentions, contributed towards the organization and administration of the government the best exertions of which a very fallible judgment was capable. Not unconscious, in the outset, of the inferiority of my qualifications, experience in my own eyes, perhaps still more in the eyes of others, has strengthened the motives to diffidence of myself; and every day the increasing weight of years admonishes me more and more, that the shade of retirement is as necessary to me as it will be welcome. Satisfied, that, if any circumstances have given peculiar value to my services, they were temporary, I have the consolation to believe, that, while choice and prudence invite me to quit the political scene, patriotism does not forbid it.

In looking forward to the moment, which is intended to terminate the career of my public life, my feelings do not permit me to suspend the deep acknowledgment of that debt of gratitude, which I owe to my beloved country for the many honors it has conferred upon me; still more for the steadfast confidence with which it has supported me; and for the opportunities I have thence enjoyed of manifesting my inviolable attachment, by services faithful and persevering, though in usefulness unequal to my zeal. If benefits have resulted to our country from these services, let it always be remembered to your praise, and as an instructive example in our annals, that under circumstances in which the passions, agitated in every direction, were liable to mislead, amidst appearances sometimes dubious, vicissitudes of fortune often discouraging, in situations in which not unfrequently want of success has countenanced the spirit of criticism, the constancy of your support was the essential prop of the efforts, and a guarantee of the plans by which they were effected. Profoundly penetrated with this idea, I shall carry it with me to my grave, as a strong incitement to unceasing vows that Heaven may continue to you the choicest tokens of its beneficence; that your union and brotherly affection may be perpetual; that the free constitution, which is the work of your hands, may be sacredly maintained; that its administration in every department may be stamped with wisdom and virtue; than, in fine, the happiness of the people of these States, under the auspices of liberty, may be made complete, by so careful a preservation and so prudent a use of this blessing, as will acquire to them the glory of recommending it to the applause, the affection, and adoption of every nation, which is yet a stranger to it.

Here, perhaps I ought to stop. But a solicitude for your welfare which cannot end but with my life, and the apprehension of danger, natural to that solicitude, urge me, on an occasion like the present, to offer to your solemn contemplation, and to recommend to your frequent review, some sentiments which are the result of much reflection, of no inconsiderable observation, and which appear to me all-important to the permanency of your felicity as a people. These will be offered to you with the more freedom, as you can only see in them the disinterested warnings of a parting friend, who can possibly have no personal motive to bias his counsel. Nor can I forget, as an encouragement to it, your indulgent reception of my sentiments on a former and not dissimilar occasion.

Interwoven as is the love of liberty with every ligament of your hearts, no recommendation of mine is necessary to fortify or confirm the attachment.

The unity of Government, which constitutes you one people, is also now dear to you. It is justly so; for it is a main pillar in the edifice of your real independence, the support of your tranquillity at home, your peace abroad; of your safety; of your prosperity; of that very Liberty, which you so highly prize. But as it is easy to foresee, that, from different causes and from different quarters, much pains will be taken, many artifices employed, to weaken in your minds the conviction of this truth; as this is the point in your political fortress against which the batteries of internal and external enemies will be most constantly and actively (though often covertly and insidiously) directed, it is of infinite moment, that you should properly estimate the immense value of your national Union to your collective and individual happiness; that you should cherish a cordial, habitual, and immovable attachment to it; accustoming yourselves to think and speak of it as of the Palladium of your political safety and prosperity; watching for its preservation with jealous anxiety; discountenancing whatever may suggest even a suspicion, that it can in any event be abandoned; and indignantly frowning upon the first dawning of every attempt to alienate any portion of our country from the rest, or to enfeeble the sacred ties which now link together the various parts.

For this you have every inducement of sympathy and interest. Citizens, by birth or choice, of a common country, that country has a right to concentrate your affections. The name of american, which belongs to you, in your national capacity, must always exalt the just pride of Patriotism, more than any appellation derived from local discriminations. With slight shades of difference, you have the same religion, manners, habits, and political principles. You have in a common cause fought and triumphed together; the Independence and Liberty you possess are the work of joint counsels, and joint efforts, of common dangers, sufferings, and successes.

But these considerations, however powerfully they address themselves to your sensibility, are greatly outweighed by those, which apply more immediately to your interest. Here every portion of our country finds the most commanding motives for carefully guarding and preserving the Union of the whole

The North, in an unrestrained intercourse with the South, protected by the equal laws of a common government, finds, in the productions of the latter, great additional resources of maritime and commercial enterprise and precious materials of manufacturing industry. The South, in the same intercourse, benefiting by the agency of the North, sees its agriculture grow and its commerce expand. Turning partly into its own channels the seamen of the North, it finds its particular navigation invigorated; and, while it contributes, in different ways, to nourish and increase the general mass of the national navigation, it looks forward to the protection of a maritime strength, to which itself is unequally adapted. The East, in a like intercourse with the West, already finds, and in the progressive improvement of interior communications by land and water, will more and more find, a valuable vent for the commodities which it brings from abroad, or manufactures at home. The West derives from the East supplies requisite to its growth and comfort, and, what is perhaps of still greater consequence, it must of necessity owe the secure enjoyment of indispensable outlets for its own productions to the weight, influence, and the future maritime strength of the Atlantic side of the Union, directed by an indissoluble community of interest as one nation. Any other tenure by which the West can hold this essential advantage, whether derived from its own separate strength, or from an apostate and unnatural connection with any foreign power, must be intrinsically precarious.

While, then, every part of our country thus feels an immediate and particular interest in Union, all the parts combined cannot fail to find in the united mass of means and efforts greater strength, greater resource, proportionably greater security from external danger, a less frequent interruption of their peace by foreign nations; and, what is of inestimable value, they must derive from Union an exemption from those broils and wars between themselves, which so frequently afflict neighboring countries not tied together by the same governments, which their own rivalships alone would be sufficient to produce, but which opposite foreign alliances, attachments, and intrigues would stimulate and embitter. Hence, likewise, they will avoid the necessity of those overgrown military establishments, which, under any form of government, are inauspicious to liberty, and which are to be regarded as particularly hostile to Republican Liberty. In this sense it is, that your Union ought to be considered as a main prop of your liberty, and that the love of the one ought to endear to you the preservation of the other.

These considerations speak a persuasive language to every reflecting and virtuous mind, and exhibit the continuance of the union as a primary object of Patriotic desire. Is there a doubt, whether a common government can embrace so large a sphere? Let experience solve it. To listen to mere speculation in such a case were criminal. We are authorized to hope, that a proper organization of the whole, with the auxiliary agency of governments for the respective subdivisions, will afford a happy issue to the experiment. It is well worth a fair and full experiment. With such powerful and obvious motives to Union, affecting all parts of our country, while experience shall not have demonstrated its impracticability, there will always be reason to distrust the patriotism of those, who in any quarter may endeavor to weaken its bands.

In contemplating the causes, which may disturb our Union, it occurs as matter of serious concern, that any ground should have been furnished for characterizing parties by Geographical discriminations, Northern and Southern, Atlantic and Western; whence designing men may endeavour to excite a belief, that there is a real difference of local interests and views. One of the expedients of party to acquire influence, within particular districts, is to misrepresent the opinions and aims of other districts. You cannot shield yourselves too much against the jealousies and heart-burnings, which spring from these misrepresentations; they tend to render alien to each other those, who ought to be bound together by fraternal affection. The inhabitants of our western country have lately had a useful lesson on this head; they have seen, in the negotiation by the Executive, and in the unanimous ratification by the Senate, of the treaty with Spain, and in the universal satisfaction at that event, throughout the United States, a decisive proof how unfounded were the suspicions propagated among them of a policy in the General Government and in the Atlantic States unfriendly to their interests in regard to the Mississippi; they have been witnesses to the formation of two treaties, that with Great Britain, and that with Spain, which secure to them every thing they could desire, in respect to our foreign relations, towards confirming their prosperity. Will it not be their wisdom to rely for the preservation of these advantages on the union by which they were procured? Will they not henceforth be deaf to those advisers, if such there are, who would sever them from their brethren, and connect them with aliens?

To the efficacy and permanency of your Union, a Government for the whole is indispensable. No alliances, however strict, between the parts can be an adequate substitute; they must inevitably experience the infractions and interruptions, which all alliances in all times have experienced. Sensible of this momentous truth, you have improved upon your first essay, by the adoption of a Constitution of Government better calculated than your former for an intimate Union, and for the efficacious management of your common concerns. This Government, the offspring of our own choice, uninfluenced and unawed, adopted upon full investigation and mature deliberation, completely free in its principles, in the distribution of its powers, uniting security with energy, and containing within itself a provision for its own amendment, has a just claim to your confidence and your support. Respect for its authority, compliance with its laws, acquiescence in its measures, are duties enjoined by the fundamental maxims of true Liberty. The basis of our political systems is the right of the people to make and to alter their Constitutions of Government. But the Constitution which at any time exists, till changed by an explicit and authentic act of the whole people, is sacredly obligatory upon all. The very idea of the power and the right of the people to establish Government presupposes the duty of every individual to obey the established Government.

All obstructions to the execution of the Laws, all combinations and associations, under whatever plausible character, with the real design to direct, control, counteract, or awe the regular deliberation and action of the constituted authorities, are destructive of this fundamental principle, and of fatal tendency. They serve to organize faction, to give it an artificial and extraordinary force; to put, in the place of the delegated will of the nation, the will of a party, often a small but artful and enterprising minority of the community; and, according to the alternate triumphs of different parties, to make the public administration the mirror of the ill-concerted and incongruous projects of faction, rather than the organ of consistent and wholesome plans digested by common counsels, and modified by mutual interests.

However combinations or associations of the above description may now and then answer popular ends, they are likely, in the course of time and things, to become potent engines, by which cunning, ambitious, and unprincipled men will be enabled to subvert the power of the people, and to usurp for themselves the reins of government; destroying afterwards the very engines, which have lifted them to unjust dominion.

Towards the preservation of your government, and the permanency of your present happy state, it is requisite, not only that you steadily discountenance irregular oppositions to its acknowledged authority, but also that you resist with care the spirit of innovation upon its principles, however specious the pretexts. One method of assault may be to effect, in the forms of the constitution, alterations, which will impair the energy of the system, and thus to undermine what cannot be directly overthrown. In all the changes to which you may be invited, remember that time and habit are at least as necessary to fix the true character of governments, as of other human institutions; that experience is the surest standard, by which to test the real tendency of the existing constitution of a country; that facility in changes, upon the credit of mere hypothesis and opinion, exposes to perpetual change, from the endless variety of hypothesis and opinion; and remember, especially, that, for the efficient management of our common interests, in a country so extensive as ours, a government of as much vigor as is consistent with the perfect security of liberty is indispensable. Liberty itself will find in such a government, with powers properly distributed and adjusted, its surest guardian. It is, indeed, little else than a name, where the government is too feeble to withstand the enterprises of faction, to confine each member of the society within the limits prescribed by the laws, and to maintain all in the secure and tranquil enjoyment of the rights of person and property.

I have already intimated to you the danger of parties in the state, with particular reference to the founding of them on geographical discriminations. Let me now take a more comprehensive view, and warn you in the most solemn manner against the baneful effects of the spirit of party, generally.

This spirit, unfortunately, is inseparable from our nature, having its root in the strongest passions of the human mind. It exists under different shapes in all governments, more or less stifled, controlled, or repressed; but, in those of the popular form, it is seen in its greatest rankness, and is truly their worst enemy.

The alternate domination of one faction over another, sharpened by the spirit of revenge, natural to party dissension, which in different ages and countries has perpetrated the most horrid enormities, is itself a frightful despotism. But this leads at length to a more formal and permanent despotism. The disorders and miseries, which result, gradually incline the minds of men to seek security and repose in the absolute power of an individual; and sooner or later the chief of some prevailing faction, more able or more fortunate than his competitors, turns this disposition to the purposes of his own elevation, on the ruins of Public Liberty.

Without looking forward to an extremity of this kind, (which nevertheless ought not to be entirely out of sight,) the common and continual mischiefs of the spirit of party are sufficient to make it the interest and duty of a wise people to discourage and restrain it.

It serves always to distract the Public Councils, and enfeeble the Public Administration. It agitates the Community with ill-founded jealousies and false alarms; kindles the animosity of one part against another, foments occasionally riot and insurrection. It opens the door to foreign influence and corruption, which find a facilitated access to the government itself through the channels of party passions. Thus the policy and the will of one country are subjected to the policy and will of another.

There is an opinion, that parties in free countries are useful checks upon the administration of the Government, and serve to keep alive the spirit of Liberty. This within certain limits is probably true; and in Governments of a Monarchical cast, Patriotism may look with indulgence, if not with favor, upon the spirit of party. But in those of the popular character, in Governments purely elective, it is a spirit not to be encouraged. From their natural tendency, it is certain there will always be enough of that spirit for every salutary purpose. And, there being constant danger of excess, the effort ought to be, by force of public opinion, to mitigate and assuage it. A fire not to be quenched, it demands a uniform vigilance to prevent its bursting into a flame, lest, instead of warming, it should consume.

It is important, likewise, that the habits of thinking in a free country should inspire caution, in those intrusted with its administration, to confine themselves within their respective constitutional spheres, avoiding in the exercise of the powers of one department to encroach upon another. The spirit of encroachment tends to consolidate the powers of all the departments in one, and thus to create, whatever the form of government, a real despotism. A just estimate of that love of power, and proneness to abuse it, which predominates in the human heart, is sufficient to satisfy us of the truth of this position. The necessity of reciprocal checks in the exercise of political power, by dividing and distributing it into different depositories, and constituting each the Guardian of the Public Weal against invasions by the others, has been evinced by experiments ancient and modern; some of them in our country and under our own eyes. To preserve them must be as necessary as to institute them. If, in the opinion of the people, the distribution or modification of the constitutional powers be in any particular wrong, let it be corrected by an amendment in the way, which the constitution designates. But let there be no change by usurpation; for, though this, in one instance, may be the instrument of good, it is the customary weapon by which free governments are destroyed. The precedent must always greatly overbalance in permanent evil any partial or transient benefit, which the use can at any time yield.

Of all the dispositions and habits, which lead to political prosperity, Religion and Morality are indispensable supports. In vain would that man claim the tribute of Patriotism, who should labor to subvert these great pillars of human happiness, these firmest props of the duties of Men and Citizens. The mere Politician, equally with the pious man, ought to respect and to cherish them. A volume could not trace all their connexions with private and public felicity. Let it simply be asked, Where is the security for property, for reputation, for life, if the sense of religious obligation desert the oaths, which are the instruments of investigation in Courts of Justice? And let us with caution indulge the supposition, that morality can be maintained without religion. Whatever may be conceded to the influence of refined education on minds of peculiar structure, reason and experience both forbid us to expect, that national morality can prevail in exclusion of religious principle.

It is substantially true, that virtue or morality is a necessary spring of popular government. The rule, indeed, extends with more or less force to every species of free government. Who, that is a sincere friend to it, can look with indifference upon attempts to shake the foundation of the fabric?

Promote, then, as an object of primary importance, institutions for the general diffusion of knowledge. In proportion as the structure of a government gives force to public opinion, it is essential that public opinion should be enlightened.

As a very important source of strength and security, cherish public credit. One method of preserving it is, to use it as sparingly as possible; avoiding occasions of expense by cultivating peace, but remembering also that timely disbursements to prepare for danger frequently prevent much greater disbursements to repel it; avoiding likewise the accumulation of debt, not only by shunning occasions of expense, but by vigorous exertions in time of peace to discharge the debts, which unavoidable wars may have occasioned, not ungenerously throwing upon posterity the burthen, which we ourselves ought to bear. The execution of these maxims belongs to your representatives, but it is necessary that public opinion should cooperate. To facilitate to them the performance of their duty, it is essential that you should practically bear in mind, that towards the payment of debts there must be Revenue; that to have Revenue there must be taxes; that no taxes can be devised, which are not more or less inconvenient and unpleasant; that the intrinsic embarrassment, inseparable from the selection of the proper objects (which is always a choice of difficulties), ought to be a decisive motive for a candid construction of the conduct of the government in making it, and for a spirit of acquiescence in the measures for obtaining revenue, which the public exigencies may at any time dictate.

Observe good faith and justice towards all Nations; cultivate peace and harmony with all. Religion and Morality enjoin this conduct; and can it be, that good policy does not equally enjoin it? It will be worthy of a free, enlightened, and, at no distant period, a great Nation, to give to mankind the magnanimous and too novel example of a people always guided by an exalted justice and benevolence. Who can doubt, that, in the course of time and things, the fruits of such a plan would richly repay any temporary advantages, which might be lost by a steady adherence to it ? Can it be, that Providence has not connected the permanent felicity of a Nation with its Virtue?

The experiment, at least, is recommended by every sentiment which ennobles human nature. Alas! is it rendered impossible by its vices?

In the execution of such a plan, nothing is more essential, than that permanent, inveterate antipathies against particular Nations, and passionate attachments for others, should be excluded; and that, in place of them, just and amicable feelings towards all should be cultivated. The Nation, which indulges towards another an habitual hatred, or an habitual fondness, is in some degree a slave. It is a slave to its animosity or to its affection, either of which is sufficient to lead it astray from its duty and its interest. Antipathy in one nation against another disposes each more readily to offer insult and injury, to lay hold of slight causes of umbrage, and to be haughty and intractable, when accidental or trifling occasions of dispute occur. Hence frequent collisions, obstinate, envenomed, and bloody contests. The Nation, prompted by ill-will and resentment, sometimes impels to war the Government, contrary to the best calculations of policy. The Government sometimes participates in the national propensity, and adopts through passion what reason would reject; at other times, it makes the animosity of the nation subservient to projects of hostility instigated by pride, ambition, and other sinister and pernicious motives. The peace often, sometimes perhaps the liberty, of Nations has been the victim.

So likewise, a passionate attachment of one Nation for another produces a variety of evils. Sympathy for the favorite Nation, facilitating the illusion of an imaginary common interest, in cases where no real common interest exists, and infusing into one the enmities of the other, betrays the former into a participation in the quarrels and wars of the latter, without adequate inducement or justification. It leads also to concessions to the favorite Nation of privileges denied to others, which is apt doubly to injure the Nation making the concessions; by unnecessarily parting with what ought to have been retained; and by exciting jealousy, ill-will, and a disposition to retaliate, in the parties from whom equal privileges are withheld. And it gives to ambitious, corrupted, or deluded citizens, (who devote themselves to the favorite nation,) facility to betray or sacrifice the interests of their own country, without odium, sometimes even with popularity; gilding, with the appearances of a virtuous sense of obligation, a commendable deference for public opinion, or a laudable zeal for public good, the base or foolish compliances of ambition, corruption, or infatuation.

As avenues to foreign influence in innumerable ways, such attachments are particularly alarming to the truly enlightened and independent Patriot. How many opportunities do they afford to tamper with domestic factions, to practise the arts of seduction, to mislead public opinion, to influence or awe the Public Councils! Such an attachment of a small or weak, towards a great and powerful nation, dooms the former to be the satellite of the latter.

Against the insidious wiles of foreign influence (I conjure you to believe me, fellow-citizens,) the jealousy of a free people ought to be constantly awake; since history and experience prove, that foreign influence is one of the most baneful foes of Republican Government. But that jealousy, to be useful, must be impartial; else it becomes the instrument of the very influence to be avoided, instead of a defence against it. Excessive partiality for one foreign nation, and excessive dislike of another, cause those whom they actuate to see danger only on one side, and serve to veil and even second the arts of influence on the other. Real patriots, who may resist the intrigues of the favorite, are liable to become suspected and odious; while its tools and dupes usurp the applause and confidence of the people, to surrender their interests.

The great rule of conduct for us, in regard to foreign nations, is, in extending our commercial relations, to have with them as little political connexion as possible. So far as we have already formed engagements, let them be fulfilled with perfect good faith. Here let us stop.

Europe has a set of primary interests, which to us have none, or a very remote relation. Hence she must be engaged in frequent controversies, the causes of which are essentially foreign to our concerns. Hence, therefore, it must be unwise in us to implicate ourselves, by artificial ties, in the ordinary vicissitudes of her politics, or the ordinary combinations and collisions of her friendships or enmities.

Our detached and distant situation invites and enables us to pursue a different course. If we remain one people, under an efficient government, the period is not far off, when we may defy material injury from external annoyance; when we may take such an attitude as will cause the neutrality, we may at any time resolve upon, to be scrupulously respected; when belligerent nations, under the impossibility of making acquisitions upon us, will not lightly hazard the giving us provocation; when we may choose peace or war, as our interest, guided by justice, shall counsel.

Why forego the advantages of so peculiar a situation? Why quit our own to stand upon foreign ground? Why, by interweaving our destiny with that of any part of Europe, entangle our peace and prosperity in the toils of European ambition, rivalship, interest, humor, or caprice?

It is our true policy to steer clear of permanent alliances with any portion of the foreign world; so far, I mean, as we are now at liberty to do it; for let me not be understood as capable of patronizing infidelity to existing engagements. I hold the maxim no less applicable to public than to private affairs, that honesty is always the best policy. I repeat it, therefore, let those engagements be observed in their genuine sense. But, in my opinion, it is unnecessary and would be unwise to extend

188

them.

Taking care always to keep ourselves, by suitable establishments, on a respectable defensive posture, we may safely trust to temporary alliances for extraordinary emergencies.

Harmony, liberal intercourse with all nations, are recommended by policy, humanity, and interest. But even our commercial policy should hold an equal and impartial hand; neither seeking nor granting exclusive favors or preferences; consulting the natural course of things; diffusing and diversifying by gentle means the streams of commerce, but forcing nothing; establishing, with powers so disposed, in order to give trade a stable course, to define the rights of our merchants, and to enable the government to support them, conventional rules of intercourse, the best that present circumstances and mutual opinion will permit, but temporary, and liable to be from time to time abandoned or varied, as experience and circumstances shall dictate; constantly keeping in view, that it is folly in one nation to look for disinterested favors from another; that it must pay with a portion of its independence for whatever it may accept under that character; that, by such acceptance, it may place itself in the condition of having given equivalents for nominal favors, and yet of being reproached with ingratitude for not giving more. There can be no greater error than to expect or calculate upon real favors from nation to nation. It is an illusion, which experience must cure, which a just pride ought to discard.

In offering to you, my countrymen, these counsels of an old and affectionate friend, I dare not hope they will make the strong and lasting impression I could wish; that they will control the usual current of the passions, or prevent our nation from running the course, which has hitherto marked the destiny of nations. But, if I may even flatter myself, that they may be productive of some partial benefit, some occasional good; that they may now and then recur to moderate the fury of party spirit, to warn against the mischiefs of foreign intrigue, to guard against the impostures of pretended patriotism; this hope will be a full recompense for the solicitude for your welfare, by which they have been dictated.

How far in the discharge of my official duties, I have been guided by the principles which have been delineated, the public records and other evidences of my conduct must witness to you and to the world. To myself, the assurance of my own conscience is, that I have at least believed myself to be guided by them.

In relation to the still subsisting war in Europe, my Proclamation of the 22nd of April 1793, is the index to my Plan. Sanctioned by your approving voice, and by that of your representatives in both Houses of Congress, the spirit of that measure has continually governed me, uninfluenced by any attempts to deter or divert me from it.

After deliberate examination, with the aid of the best lights I could obtain, I was well satisfied that our country, under all the circumstances of the case, had a right to take, and was bound in duty and interest to take, a neutral position. Having taken it, I determined, as far as should depend upon me, to maintain it, with moderation, perseverance, and firmness.

The considerations, which respect the right to hold this conduct, it is not necessary on this occasion to detail. I will only observe, that, according to my understanding of the matter, that right, so far from being denied by any of the Belligerent Powers, has been virtually admitted by all.

The duty of holding a neutral conduct may

be inferred, without any thing more, from the obligation which justice and humanity impose on every nation, in cases in which it is free to act, to maintain inviolate the relations of peace and amity towards other nations.

The inducements of interest for observing that conduct will best be referred to your own reflections and experience. With me, a predominant motive has been to endeavour to gain time to our country to settle and mature its yet recent institutions, and to progress without interruption to that degree of strength and consistency, which is necessary to give it, humanly speaking, the command of its own fortunes.

Though, in reviewing the incidents of my administration, I am unconscious of intentional error, I am nevertheless too sensible of my defects not to think it probable that I may have committed many errors. Whatever they may be, I fervently beseech the Almighty to avert or mitigate the evils to which they may tend. I shall also carry with me the hope, that my Country will never cease to view them with indulgence; and that, after forty-five years of my life dedicated to its service with an upright zeal, the faults of incompetent abilities will be consigned to oblivion, as myself must soon be to the mansions of rest.

Relying on its kindness in this as in other things, and actuated by that fervent love towards it, which is so natural to a man, who views it in the native soil of himself and his progenitors for several generations; I anticipate with pleasing expectation that retreat, in which I promise myself to realize, without alloy, the sweet enjoyment of partaking, in the midst of my fellow-citizens, the benign influence of good laws under a free government, the ever favorite object of my heart, and the happy reward, as I trust, of our mutual cares, labors, and dangers.

ELIZABETH CADY STANTON
(1815–1902)

"The happiest people I have known have been those who gave themselves no concern about their own souls, but did their uttermost to mitigate the miseries of others."

Elizabeth Cady Stanton was a prominent figure in the women's movement as well as a dedicated abolitionist. She co-founded the National Woman's Suffrage Association with Susan B. Anthony in 1869. She has also written many influential works including History of Woman's Suffrage and was co-editor of The Revolution, a well-known periodical focusing on gaining suffrage for women.

ELIZABETH CADY STANTON

THE DECLARATION
OF SENTIMENTS

ON JULY 19TH AND 20TH OF 1848, Elizabeth Cady Stanton, Lucretia Mott, and several hundred American activists gathered in Seneca Falls, NY to lead one of the nation's first women's rights conventions—what would come to be known as the Seneca Falls Convention. At a point in time when slavery had become a dividing factor for our nation, many women involved in the Abolitionist movement also began to question issues of equality based on gender. Of these women who dared to question tradition, Elizabeth Cady Stanton stood proud as the speaker and author of The Declaration of Sentiments which was inspired by, and written in the style of, The Declaration of Independence.

JULY 19–20, 1848

When, in the course of human events, it becomes necessary for one portion of the

family of man to assume among the people of
the earth a position different from that which
they have hitherto occupied, but one to which
the laws of nature and of nature's God entitle
them, a decent respect to the opinions of mankind requires that they should declare the
causes that impel them to such a course.

We hold these truths to be self-evident:
that all men and women are created equal;
that they are endowed by their Creator with
certain inalienable rights; that among these
are life, liberty, and the pursuit of happiness;
that to secure these rights governments are
instituted, deriving their just powers from
the consent of the governed. Whenever any
form of government becomes destructive of
these ends, it is the right of those who suffer from it to refuse allegiance to it, and to
insist upon the institution of a new government, laying its foundation on such principles,
and organizing its powers in such form, as to
them shall seem most likely to effect their
safety and happiness. Prudence, indeed, will
dictate that governments long established
should not be changed for light and transient causes; and accordingly all experience
hath shown that mankind are more disposed
to suffer. while evils are sufferable, than to

right themselves by abolishing the forms to which they are accustomed. But when a long train of abuses and usurpations, pursuing invariably the same object, evinces a design to reduce them under absolute despotism, it is their duty to throw off such government, and to provide new guards for their future security. Such has been the patient sufferance of the women under this government, and such is now the necessity which constrains them to demand the equal station to which they are entitled. The history of mankind is a history of repeated injuries and usurpations on the part of man toward woman, having in direct object the establishment of an absolute tyranny over her. To prove this, let facts be submitted to a candid world.

The history of mankind is a history of repeated injuries and usurpations on the part of man toward woman, having in direct object the establishment of an absolute tyranny over her. To prove this, let facts be submitted to a candid world.

He has never permitted her to exercise her inalienable right to the elective franchise.

He has compelled her to submit to laws, in the formation of which she had no voice.

He has withheld from her rights which

are given to the most ignorant and degraded men—both natives and foreigners.

Having deprived her of this first right of a citizen, the elective franchise, thereby leaving her without representation in the halls of legislation, he has oppressed her on all sides.

He has made her, if married, in the eye of the law, civilly dead.

He has taken from her all right in property, even to the wages she earns.

He has made her, morally, an irresponsible being, as she can commit many crimes with impunity, provided they be done in the presence of her husband. In the covenant of marriage, she is compelled to promise obedience to her husband, he becoming, to all intents and purposes, her master—the law giving him power to deprive her of her liberty, and to administer chastisement.

He has so framed the laws of divorce, as to what shall be the proper causes, and in case of separation, to whom the guardianship of the children shall be given, as to be wholly regardless of the happiness of women—the law, in all cases, going upon a false supposition of the supremacy of man, and giving all power into his hands.

After depriving her of all rights as a married woman, if single, and the owner of property, he has taxed her to support a government which recognizes her only when her property can be made profitable to it.

He has monopolized nearly all the profitable employments, and from those she is permitted to follow, she receives but a scanty remuneration. He closes against her all the avenues to wealth and distinction which he considers most honorable to himself. As a teacher of theology, medicine, or law, she is not known.

He has denied her the facilities for obtaining a thorough education, all colleges being closed against her.

He allows her in church, as well as state, but a subordinate position, claiming apostolic authority for her exclusion from the ministry, and, with some exceptions, from any public participation in the affairs of the church.

He has created a false public sentiment by giving to the world a different code of morals for men and women, by which moral delinquencies which exclude women from society, are not only tolerated, but deemed of little account in man.

He has usurped the prerogative of Jehovah himself, claiming it as his right to assign for her a sphere of action, when that belongs to her conscience and to her God.

He has endeavored, in every way that he could, to destroy her conficence in her own powers, to lessen her self-respect, and to make her willing to lead a dependent and abject life.

Now, in view of this entire disfranchisement of one-half the people of this country, their social and religious degradation—in view of the unjust laws above mentioned, and because women do feel themselves aggrieved, oppressed, and fraudulently deprived of their most sacred rights, we insist that they have immediate admission to all the rights and privileges which belong to them as citizens of the United States.

SOJOURNER TRUTH
(1797–1883)

———————

"Those are the same stars, and that is the same moon, that look down upon your brothers and sisters, and which they see as they look up to them, though they are ever so far away from us, and each other."

———————

Sojourner Truth was born into slavery, later gaining her freedom in 1827 when New York began the process of emancipation. She then traveled around the country delivering speeches on woman's rights and abolition and came to be an influential activist in both movements.

SOJOURNER TRUTH
Ain't I a Woman?

At the 1851 Women's Rights Convention in Akron, Ohio, Sojourner Truth delivered this speech in which she unveiled the hypocrisies of racial and gender subordination that existed throughout the 19th century. It was later recorded as follows by Marcus Robinson, who had worked closely with Truth. In 1863, the speech was transformed by Frances Gage, an organizer of the Convention, and came to be known as the "Ain't I a Woman?" speech.

MAY 1851

*The following is the original 1851 report
by Marcus Robinson.*

One of the most unique and interesting speeches of the convention was made by Sojourner Truth, an emancipated slave. It is impossible to transfer it to paper, or convey any adequate idea of the effect it produced upon the audience. Those only can appreciate it who saw her powerful form, her whole-souled, earnest gesture, and listened to her strong and truthful tones. She came forward to the platform and addressing the President said with great simplicity: "May I say a few words?" Receiving an affirmative answer, she proceeded:

I want to say a few words about this matter. I am a woman's rights. I have as much muscle as any man, and can do as much work as any man. I have plowed and reaped and husked and chopped and mowed, and can any man do more than that? I have heard much about the sexes being equal. I can carry as much as any man, and can eat as much too, if I can get it. I am as strong as any man that is now. As for intellect, all I can say is, if a woman have a pint, and a man a quart -- why can't she have her little pint full? You need not be afraid to give us our rights for fear we will take too much, -- for we can't take more than our pint'll hold. The poor men seems to be all in confusion, and don't know what to do. Why children, if you have woman's rights, give it to her and you will feel better. You will have your own rights, and they won't be so much trouble. I can't read, but I can hear. I have heard the bible and have learned that Eve caused man to sin. Well, if woman upset the world, do give her a chance to set it right side up again. The Lady has spoken about Jesus, how he never spurned woman from him, and she was right. When Lazarus died, Mary and Martha came to him with faith and love and besought him to raise their brother. And Jesus wept and Lazarus came forth. And how came Jesus into the world? Through God who created him and the woman who bore him. Man, where was your part? But the women are coming up blessed be God and a few of the men are coming up with them. But man is in a tight place, the poor slave is on him, woman is coming on him, he is surely between a hawk and a buzzard.

ABRAHAM LINCOLN
(1809–1865)

"A house divided against itself
cannot stand."

Abraham Lincoln, our country's sixteenth President, delivered The Gettysburg Address not long before he was re-elected for second term, in 1864. Less than one month after delivering his second inaugural address (his favorite speech), Lincoln was assassinated. Yet his accomplishments as president, and his powerful insights about the American spirit, shaped history and continue to resonate with Americans to this day.

ABRAHAM LINCOLN
THE GETTYSBURG ADDRESS

FOUR MONTHS AFTER THE DEFEAT of the Confederate armies at the Battle of Gettysburg, President Abraham Lincoln delivered what would come to be known as one of the greatest speeches in American history. Delivered during the dedication of the Soldiers' National Cemetery in Gettysburg, Pennsylvania, before the end of Civil War, the speech lasted just over two minutes, yet its magnitude has endured for generations. The Gettysburg Address served to bring meaning and dedication to those who lost their lives during the Civil War, while also instilling in Americans the duty to guard freedom and equality for all mankind.

NOVEMBER 19, 1863

Four score and seven years ago our fathers brought forth on this continent, a new nation, conceived in Liberty, and dedicated to the proposition that all men are created equal.

Now we are engaged in a great civil war, testing whether that nation, or any nation so conceived and so dedicated, can long endure. We are met on a great battle-field of that war. We have come to dedicate a portion of that field, as a final resting place for those who here gave their lives that that nation might live. It is altogether fitting and proper that we should do this.

But, in a larger sense, we cannot dedicate—we cannot consecrate—we cannot hallow—this ground. The brave men, living and dead, who struggled here, have consecrated it, far above our poor power to add or detract. The world will little note, nor long remember what we say here, but it can never forget what they did here. It is for us the living, rather, to be dedicated here to the unfinished work which they who fought here have thus far so nobly advanced. It is rather for us to be here dedicated to the great task remaining before us—that from these honored dead we take increased devotion to that cause for which they gave the last full measure of devotion—that we here highly resolve that these dead shall not have died in vain—that this nation, under God, shall have a new birth of freedom—and that government of the people, by the people, for the people, shall not perish from the earth.

FRANKLIN D. ROOSEVELT

(1882–1945)

———————

"The test of our progress is not whether we add more to the abundance of those who have much; it is whether we provide enough for those who have too little."

———————

Franklin D. Roosevelt was our nation's thirty-second President and is the only U.S. President to have served more than two terms. He created the New Deal during the Great Depression which provided unemployment relief and economic reform. His economic programs (such as the FDIC) developed during this time continue to play key roles in our nation's commerce.

FRANKLIN DELANO ROOSEVELT

THE FOUR FREEDOMS

IN HIS 1941 State of the Union Address, Franklin Delano Roosevelt delivered his *Four Freedoms* speech in which he outlined the four most essential freedoms to be granted to all human beings—freedom of speech and expression, freedom of religion, freedom from want, and freedom from fear. It is within this speech that President Roosevelt had sparked in Americans the resolve to protect the integrity and longevity of the democratic system that America has come to represent.

JANUARY 6, 1941

Mr. President, Mr. Speaker, members of the 77th Congress:

I address you, the members of this new Congress, at a moment unprecedented in the history of the union. I use the word "unprecedented" because at no previous time has American security been as seriously threatened from without as it is today.

Since the permanent formation of our government under the Constitution in 1789, most of the periods of crisis in our history have related to our domestic affairs. And, fortunately, only one of these—the four-year war between the States—ever threatened our national unity. Today, thank God, 130,000,000 Americans in 48 States have forgotten points of the compass in our national unity.

It is true that prior to 1914 the United States often has been disturbed by events in other continents. We have even engaged in two wars with European nations and in a number of undeclared wars in the West Indies, in the Mediterranean and in the Pacific, for the maintenance of American rights and for the principles of peaceful commerce. But in no case had a serious threat been raised against our national safety or our continued independence.

What I seek to convey is the historic truth that the United States as a nation has at all times maintained opposition—clear, definite opposition—to any attempt to lock us in behind an ancient Chinese wall while the procession of civilization went past. Today, thinking of our children and of their children, we oppose enforced isolation for ourselves or for any other part of the Americas.

That determination of ours, extending over all these years, was proved, for example, in the early days during the quarter century of wars following the French Revolution. While the Napoleonic struggles did threaten interests of the United States because of the French foothold in the West Indies and in Louisiana, and while we engaged in the War of 1812 to vindicate our right to peaceful trade, it is nevertheless clear that neither France nor Great Britain nor any other nation was aiming at domination of the whole world.

And in like fashion, from 1815 to 1914—ninety-nine years—no single war in Europe or in Asia constituted a real threat against our future or against the future of any other American nation.

Except in the Maximilian interlude in Mexico, no foreign power sought to establish itself in this hemisphere. And the strength of the British fleet in the Atlantic has been a friendly strength; it is still a friendly strength.

Even when the World War broke out in 1914, it seemed to contain only small threat of danger to our own American future. But as time went on, as we remember, the American people began to visualize what the downfall of democratic nations might mean to our own democracy.

We need not overemphasize imperfections in the peace of Versailles. We need not harp on failure of the democracies to deal with problems of world reconstruction. We should remember that the peace of 1919 was far less unjust than the kind of pacification which began even before Munich, and which is being carried on under the new order of tyranny that seeks to spread over every continent today. The American people have unalterably set their faces against that tyranny.

I suppose that every realist knows that the democratic way of life is at this moment being directly assailed in every part of the world— assailed either by arms or by secret spreading of poisonous propaganda by those who seek to destroy unity and promote discord in nations that are still at peace. During 16 long months this assault has blotted out the whole pattern of democratic life in an appalling number of independent nations, great and small. And the assailants are still on the march, threatening other nations, great and small.

Therefore, as your President, performing my constitutional duty to "give to the Congress information of the state of the union," I find it unhappily necessary to report that the future and the safety of our country and of our democracy are overwhelmingly involved in events far beyond our borders.

Armed defense of democratic existence is now being gallantly waged in four continents. If that defense fails, all the population and all the resources of Europe and Asia, and Africa and Austral-Asia will be dominated by conquerors. And let us remember that the total of those populations in those four continents, the total of those populations and their resources greatly exceed the sum total of the population and the resources of the whole of the Western Hemisphere—yes, many times over.

In times like these it is immature—and, incidentally, untrue—for anybody to brag that an unprepared America, single-handed and with one hand tied behind its back, can hold off the whole world.

No realistic American can expect from a

216

dictator's peace international generosity, or return of true independence, or world disarmament, or freedom of expression, or freedom of religion—or even good business. Such a peace would bring no security for us or for our neighbors. Those who would give up essential liberty to purchase a little temporary safety deserve neither liberty nor safety.

As a nation we may take pride in the fact that we are soft-hearted; but we cannot afford to be soft-headed. We must always be wary of those who with sounding brass and a tinkling cymbal preach the "ism" of appeasement. We must especially beware of that small group of selfish men who would clip the wings of the American eagle in order to feather their own nests.

I have recently pointed out how quickly the tempo of modern warfare could bring into our very midst the physical attack which we must eventually expect if the dictator nations win this war.

There is much loose talk of our immunity from immediate and direct invasion from across the seas. Obviously, as long as the British Navy retains its power, no such danger exists. Even if there were no British Navy, it is not probable that any enemy would be stupid enough to attack us by landing troops in the United States from across thousands of miles of ocean, until it had acquired strategic bases from which to operate.

But we learn much from the lessons of the past years in Europe—particularly the lesson of Norway, whose essential seaports were captured by treachery and surprise built up over a series of years. The first phase of the invasion of this hemisphere would not be the landing of regular troops. The necessary strategic points would be occupied by secret agents and by their dupes—and great numbers of them are already here and in Latin America. As long as the aggressor nations maintain the offensive they, not we, will choose the time and the place and the method of their attack.

And that is why the future of all the American Republics is today in serious danger. That is why this annual message to the Congress is unique in our history. That is why every member of the executive branch of the government and every member of the Congress face great responsibility, great accountability. The need of the moment is that our actions and our policy should be devoted primarily—almost exclusively—to meeting this foreign pril. For all our domestic problems are now a part of the great emergency.

Just as our national policy in internal affairs has been based upon a decent respect for the rights and the dignity of all our fellow men within our gates, so our national policy in foreign affairs has been based on a decent respect for the rights and the dignity of all nations, large and small. And the justice of morality must and will win in the end.

Our national policy is this:

First, by an impressive expression of the public will and without regard to partisanship, we are committed to all-inclusive national defense.

Secondly, by an impressive expression of the public will and without regard to partisanship, we are committed to full support of all those resolute people everywhere who are resisting aggression and are thereby keeping war away from our hemisphere. By this support we express our determination that the democratic cause shall prevail, and we strengthen the defense and the security of our own nation.

Third, by an impressive expression of the public will and without regard to partisanship, we are committed to the proposition that principles of morality and considerations for our own security will never permit us to acquiesce in a peace dictated by aggressors and sponsored by appeasers. We know that enduring peace cannot be bought at the cost of other people's freedom.

In the recent national election there was no substantial difference between the two great parties in respect to that national policy. No issue was fought out on this line before the American electorate. And today it is abundantly evident that American citizens everywhere are demanding and supporting speedy and complete action in recognition of obvious danger.

Therefore, the immediate need is a swift and driving increase in our armament production. Leaders of industry and labor have responded to our summons. Goals of speed have been set. In some cases these goals are being reached ahead of time. In some cases we are on schedule; in other cases there are slight but not serious delays. And in some cases—and, I am sorry to say, very important cases—we are all concerned by the slowness of the accomplishment of our plans.

The Army and Navy, however, have made

"Any society that would give up a little liberty to gain a little security will deserve neither and lose both."

—BENJAMIN FRANKLIN (1706–1790)
Founding Father, Inventor, and Author

substantial progress during the past year. Actual experience is improving and speeding up our methods of production with every passing day. And today's best is not good enough for tomorrow.

I am not satisfied with the progress thus far made. The men in charge of the program represent the best in training, in ability, and in patriotism. They are not satisfied with the progress thus far made. None of us will be satisfied until the job is done.

No matter whether the original goal was set too high or too low, our objective is quicker and better results.

To give you two illustrations:

We are behind schedule in turning out finished airplanes. We are working day and night to solve the innumerable problems and to catch up.

We are ahead of schedule in building warships, but we are working to get even further ahead of that schedule.

To change a whole nation from a basis of peacetime production of implements of peace to a basis of wartime production of implements of war is no small task. And the greatest difficulty comes at the beginning of the program, when new tools, new plant facilities, new assembly lines, new shipways must first be constructed before the actual material begins to flow steadily and speedily from them.

The Congress of course, must rightly keep itself informed at all times of the progress of the program. However, there is certain information, as the Congress itself will readily recognize, which, in the interests of our own security and those of the nations that we are supporting, must of needs be kept in confidence.

New circumstances are constantly begetting new needs for our safety. I shall ask this Congress for greatly increased new appropriations and authorizations to carry on what we have begun.

I also ask this Congress for authority and for funds sufficient to manufacture additional munitions and war supplies of many kinds, to be turned over to those nations which are now in actual war with aggressor nations. Our most useful and immediate role is to act as an arsenal for them as well as for ourselves. They do not need manpower, but they do need billions of dollars' worth of the weapons of defense.

The time is near when they will not be able to pay for them all in ready cash. We cannot, and we will not, tell them that they must sur-render merely because of present inability to pay for the weapons which we know they must have.

I do not recommend that we make them a loan of dollars with which to pay for these weapons—a loan to be repaid in dollars. I rec-ommend that we make it possible for those nations to continue to obtain war materials in the United States, fitting their orders into our own program. And nearly all of their material would, if the time ever came, be useful in our own defense.

Taking counsel of expert military and naval authorities, considering what is best for our own security, we are free to decide how much should be kept here and how much should be sent abroad to our friends who, by their determined and heroic resistance, are giving us time in which to make ready our own defense.

For what we send abroad we shall be repaid, repaid within a reasonable time fol-lowing the close of hostilities, repaid in simi-lar materials, or at our option in other goods of many kinds which they can produce and which we need.

Let us say to the democracies: "We Americans are vitally concerned in your defense of freedom. We are putting forth our energies, our resources, and our organizing powers to give you the strength to regain and maintain a free world. We shall send you in ever-increasing numbers, ships, planes, tanks, guns. That is our purpose and our pledge."

In fulfillment of this purpose we will not be intimidated by the threats of dictators that they will regard as a breach of international law or as an act of war our aid to the democracies which dare to resist their aggression. Such aid—Such aid is not an act of war, even if a dictator should unilaterally proclaim it so to be.

And when the dictators—if the dictators—are ready to make war upon us, they will not wait for an act of war on our part.

They did not wait for Norway or Belgium or the Netherlands to commit an act of war. Their only interest is in a new one-way international law, which lacks mutuality in its observance and therefore becomes an instrument of oppression. The happiness of future generations of Americans may well depend on how effective and how immediate we can make our aid felt. No one can tell the exact character of the emergency situations that we may be called upon to meet. The nation's hands must not be tied when the nation's life is in danger.

Yes, and we must prepare, all of us prepare, to make the sacrifices that the emergency—almost as serious as war itself—demands. Whatever stands in the way of speed and efficiency in defense, in defense preparations of any kind, must give way to the national need.

A free nation has the right to expect full cooperation from all groups. A free nation has the right to look to the leaders of business, of labor, and of agriculture to take the lead in stimulating effort, not among other groups but within their own group.

The best way of dealing with the few slackers or trouble-makers in our midst is, first, to shame them by patriotic example, and if that fails, to use the sovereignty of government to save government.

As men do not live by bread alone, they do not fight by armaments alone. Those who man our defenses and those behind them who build our defenses must have the stamina and the courage which come from unshakable belief in the manner of life which they are defending.

"Real freedom lies in wildness,
not in civilization."

—CHARLES LINDBERGH (1902–1974)
*Aviator, and recipient of the
Medal of Honor in 1927*

The mighty action that we are calling for cannot be based on a disregard of all the things worth fighting for.

The nation takes great satisfaction and much strength from the things which have been done to make its people conscious of their individual stake in the preservation of democratic life in America. Those things have toughened the fiber of our people, have renewed their faith and strengthened their devotion to the institutions we make ready to protect.

Certainly this is no time for any of us to stop thinking about the social and economic problems which are the root cause of the social revolution which is today a supreme factor in the world. For there is nothing mysterious about the foundations of a healthy and strong democracy.

The basic things expected by our people of their political and economic systems are simple. They are:

· Equality of opportunity for youth and for others.

· Jobs for those who can work.

· Security for those who need it.

- The ending of special privilege for the few.

- The preservation of civil liberties for all.

- The enjoyment—The enjoyment of the fruits of scientific progress in a wider and constantly rising standard of living.

These are the simple, the basic things that must never be lost sight of in the turmoil and unbelievable complexity of our modern world. The inner and abiding strength of our economic and political systems is dependent upon the degree to which they fulfill these expectations.

Many subjects connected with our social economy call for immediate improvement. As examples:

We should bring more citizens under the coverage of old-age pensions and unemployment insurance.

We should widen the opportunities for adequate medical care.

We should plan a better system by which persons deserving or needing gainful employment may obtain it.

I have called for personal sacrifice, and I am assured of the willingness of almost all

Americans to respond to that call. A part of the sacrifice means the payment of more money in taxes. In my budget message I will recommend that a greater portion of this great defense program be paid for from taxation than we are paying for today. No person should try, or be allowed to get rich out of the program, and the principle of tax payments in accordance with ability to pay should be constantly before our eyes to guide our legislation.

If the Congress maintains these principles the voters, putting patriotism ahead of pocketbooks, will give you their applause.

In the future days, which we seek to make secure, we look forward to a world founded upon four essential human freedoms.

The first is freedom of speech and expression—everywhere in the world.

The second is freedom of every person to worship God in his own way—everywhere in the world.

The third is freedom from want, which, translated into world terms, means economic understandings which will secure to every nation a healthy peacetime life for its inhabitants—everywhere in the world.

The fourth is freedom from fear, which,

translated into world terms, means a world-wide reduction of armaments to such a point and in such a thorough fashion that no nation will be in a position to commit an act of physical aggression against any neighbor—anywhere in the world.

That is no vision of a distant millennium. It is a definite basis for a kind of world attainable in our own time and generation. That kind of world is the very antithesis of the so-called "new order" of tyranny which the dictators seek to create with the crash of a bomb.

To that new order we oppose the greater conception—the moral order. A good society is able to face schemes of world domination and foreign revolutions alike without fear.

Since the beginning of our American history we have been engaged in change, in a perpetual, peaceful revolution, a revolution which goes on steadily, quietly, adjusting itself to changing conditions without the concentration camp or the quicklime in the ditch. The world order which we seek is the cooperation of free countries, working together in a friendly, civilized society.

This nation has placed its destiny in the hands and heads and hearts of its millions of free men and women, and its faith in freedom under the guidance of God. Freedom means the supremacy of human rights everywhere. Our support goes to those who struggle to gain those rights and keep them. Our strength is our unity of purpose.

To that high concept there can be no end save victory.

JOHN F. KENNEDY
(1917–1963)

———————————

*"Ask not what your country can do for you,
ask what you can do for your country."*

———————————

John F. Kennedy served as a commander in
World War II and later became a Member of
the House of Representatives and then Senator of Massachusetts before becoming our
nation's 35th President. Before his assassination in 1963, JFK presided over such events as
the Bay of Pigs Invasion, the Cuban Missile
Crisis, and the Civil Rights Movement. At the
age of 43, he was the youngest President to
have been elected into office and is also the
only President to have won a Pulitzer Prize.

JOHN F. KENNEDY
Inaugural Address

In one of the closest elections in American history, John F. Kennedy defeated Republican candidate Richard Nixon and came to be known by many as the embodiment of promise and, as a World War II veteran, a symbol of hope for a better future in the aftermath of one of the deadliest wars in history.

JANUARY 20, 1961

Vice President Johnson, Mr. Speaker, Mr. Chief Justice, President Eisenhower, Vice President Nixon, President Truman, reverend clergy, fellow citizens, we observe today not a victory of party, but a celebration of freedom—symbolizing an end, as well as a beginning—signifying renewal, as well as change. For I have sworn before you and Almighty God the same solemn oath our forebears prescribed nearly a century and three quarters ago.

The world is very different now. For man holds in his mortal hands the power to abolish all forms of human poverty and all forms of human life. And yet the same revolutionary beliefs for which our forebears fought are still at issue around the globe—the belief that the rights of man come not from the generosity of the state, but from the hand of God.

We dare not forget today that we are the heirs of that first revolution. Let the word go forth from this time and place, to friend and foe alike, that the torch has been passed to a new generation of Americans—born in this century, tempered by war, disciplined by a hard and bitter peace, proud of our ancient heritage—and unwilling to witness or permit the slow undoing of those human rights to which this Nation has always been committed, and to which we are committed today at home and around the world.

Let every nation know, whether it wishes us well or ill, that we shall pay any price, bear any burden, meet any hardship, support any friend, oppose any foe, in order to assure the survival and the success of liberty.

This much we pledge—and more.

To those old allies whose cultural and spiritual origins we share, we pledge the loyalty of faithful friends. United, there is little we cannot do in a host of cooperative ventures. Divided, there is little we can do—for we dare not meet a powerful challenge at odds and split asunder.

To those new States whom we welcome to the ranks of the free, we pledge our word that one form of colonial control shall not have passed away merely to be replaced by a far more iron tyranny. We shall not always expect to find them supporting our view. But we shall always hope to find them strongly supporting their own freedom—and to remember that, in the past, those who foolishly sought power by riding the back of the tiger ended up inside.

To those peoples in the huts and villages across the globe struggling to break the bonds of mass misery, we pledge our best efforts to help them help themselves, for whatever period is required—not because the Communists may be doing it, not because we seek their votes, but because it is right. If a free society cannot help the many who are poor, it cannot save the few who are rich.

To our sister republics south of our border, we offer a special pledge—to convert our good words into good deeds—in a new alliance for progress—to assist free men and free governments in casting off the chains of poverty. But this peaceful revolution of hope cannot become the prey of hostile powers. Let all our neighbors know that we shall join with them to oppose aggression or subversion anywhere in the Americas. And let every other power know that this Hemisphere intends to remain the master of its own house.

To that world assembly of sovereign states, the United Nations, our last best hope in an age where the instruments of war have far outpaced the instruments of peace, we renew our pledge of support—to prevent it from becoming merely a forum for invective—to strengthen its shield of the new and the weak—and to enlarge the area in which its writ may run.

Finally, to those nations who would make themselves our adversary, we offer not a pledge but a request: that both sides begin anew the quest for peace, before the dark powers of destruction unleashed by science engulf all humanity in planned or accidental self-destruction.

We dare not tempt them with weakness. For only when our arms are sufficient beyond doubt can we be certain beyond doubt that they will never be employed.

But neither can two great and powerful groups of nations take comfort from our present course—both sides overburdened by the cost of modern weapons, both rightly alarmed by the steady spread of the deadly atom, yet both racing to alter that uncertain balance of terror that stays the hand of mankind's final war.

So let us begin anew—remembering on both sides that civility is not a sign of weakness, and sincerity is always subject to proof. Let us never negotiate out of fear. But let us never fear to negotiate.

Let both sides explore what problems unite us instead of belaboring those problems which divide us.

Let both sides, for the first time, formulate serious and precise proposals for the inspection and control of arms—and bring the absolute power to destroy other nations under the absolute control of all nations.

Let both sides seek to invoke the wonders of science instead of its terrors. Together let us explore the stars, conquer the deserts, eradicate disease, tap the ocean depths, and encourage the arts and commerce.

Let both sides unite to heed in all corners

of the earth the command of Isaiah—to "undo the heavy burdens... and to let the oppressed go free."

And if a beachhead of cooperation may push back the jungle of suspicion, let both sides join in creating a new endeavor, not a new balance of power, but a new world of law, where the strong are just and the weak secure and the peace preserved.

All this will not be finished in the first 100 days. Nor will it be finished in the first 1,000 days, nor in the life of this Administration, nor even perhaps in our lifetime on this planet. But let us begin.

In your hands, my fellow citizens, more than in mine, will rest the final success or failure of our course. Since this country was founded, each generation of Americans has been summoned to give testimony to its national loyalty. The graves of young Americans who answered the call to service surround the globe.

Now the trumpet summons us again—not as a call to bear arms, though arms we need; not as a call to battle, though embattled we are—but a call to bear the burden of a long twilight struggle, year in and year out, "rejoicing in hope, patient in tribulation"—a struggle against the common enemies of man: tyranny, poverty, disease, and war itself.

Can we forge against these enemies a grand and global alliance, North and South, East and West, that can assure a more fruitful life for all mankind? Will you join in that historic effort?

In the long history of the world, only a few generations have been granted the role of defending freedom in its hour of maximum danger. I do not shrink from this responsibility—I welcome it. I do not believe that any of us would exchange places with any other people or any other generation. The energy, the faith, the devotion which we bring to this endeavor will light our country and all who serve it—and the glow from that fire can truly light the world.

And so, my fellow Americans: ask not what your country can do for you—ask what you can do for your country.

My fellow citizens of the world: ask not what America will do for you, but what together we can do for the freedom of man.

Finally, whether you are citizens of America or citizens of the world, ask of us the same high standards of strength and sacrifice which we ask of you. With a good conscience our only sure reward, with history the final judge of our deeds, let us go forth to lead the land we love, asking His blessing and His help, but knowing that here on earth God's work must truly be our own.

GERALD RUDOLPH FORD, JR.
(1913–2006)

"I believe that truth is the glue that holds government together, not only our government but civilization itself."

Gerald Rudolph Ford, Jr. served as Vice President under Richard Nixon before becoming our nation's 38th President upon Nixon's resignation in 1974. He also had nearly 25 years of experience working in the House of Representatives. Ford died in 2006 at the age of 93, making him the longest-lived President in U.S. history.

GERALD R. FORD

A War That is Finished

(excerpted)

Nearing the end of the Vietnam War, President Ford delivered this speech as a response to whether the United States would continue the long and violent struggle to preserve South Vietnam from the Communist powers of the North Vietnamese. Here, President Ford speaks to students at Tulane University, urging them to take pride in their role in America's future—a future in which the United States will finally have moved on from "a war that is finished as far as America is concerned."

APRIL 23, 1975

It is really a great privilege and a very high honor to have an opportunity of participating again in a student activity at Tulane University. And for this opportunity, I thank you very, very much.

Each time that I have been privileged to visit Tulane, I have come away newly impressed with the intense application of the student body to the great issues of our time, and I am pleased tonight to observe that your interest hasn't changed one bit.

When I had the privilege of speaking here in 1968 at your "Directions '68" forum, I had no idea that my own career and our entire Nation would move so soon in another direction. And I say again, I am extremely proud to be invited back.

Just as Tulane has made a great transition from the past to the future, so has New Orleans, the legendary city that has made such a unique contribution to our great America. New Orleans is more, as I see it, than weathered bricks and cast-iron balconies. It is a state of mind, a melting pot that represents the very, very best of America's evolution, an example of retention of a very special culture in a progressive environment of modern change.

On January 8, 1815, a monumental American victory was achieved here—the Battle of New Orleans. Louisiana had been a State for less than three years, but outnumbered

Americans innovated, out-numbered Americans used the tactics of the frontier to defeat a veteran British force trained in the strategy of the Napoleonic wars.

We as a nation had suffered humiliation and a measure of defeat in the War of 1812. Our National Capital in Washington had been captured and burned. So, the illustrious victory in the Battle of New Orleans was a powerful restorative to our national pride.

Yet, the victory at New Orleans actually took place two weeks after the signing of the armistice in Europe. Thousands died although a peace had been negotiated. The combatants had not gotten the word. Yet, the epic struggle nevertheless restored America's pride.

Today, America can regain the sense of pride that existed before Vietnam. But it cannot be achieved by refighting a war that is finished as far as America is concerned. As I see it, the time has come to look forward to an agenda for the future, to unify, to bind up the Nation's wounds, and to restore its health and its optimistic self-confidence.

In New Orleans, a great battle was fought after a war was over. In New Orleans tonight, we can begin a great national reconciliation.

The first engagement must be with the problems of today, but just as importantly, the problems of the future. That is why I think it is so appropriate that I find myself tonight at a university which addresses itself to preparing young people for the challenge of tomorrow.

I ask that we stop refighting the battles and the recriminations of the past. I ask that we look now at what is right with America, at our possibilities and our potentialities for change and growth and achievement and sharing. I ask that we accept the responsibilities of leadership as a good neighbor to all peoples and the enemy of none. I ask that we strive to become, in the finest American tradition, something more tomorrow than we are today.

Instead of my addressing the image of America, I prefer to consider the reality of America. It is true that we have launched our Bicentennial celebration without having achieved human perfection, but we have attained a very remarkable self-governed society that possesses the flexibility and the dynamism to grow and undertake an entirely new agenda, an agenda for America's third century.

So, I ask you to join me in helping to write that agenda. I am as determined as a President can be to seek national rediscovery of the belief in ourselves that characterized the most creative periods in our Nation 's history. The greatest challenge of creativity, as I see it, lies ahead.

We, of course, are saddened indeed by the events in Indochina. But these events, tragic as they are, portend neither the end of the world nor of America's leadership in the world.

Let me put it this way, if I might. Some tend to feel that if we do not succeed in everything everywhere, then we have succeeded in nothing anywhere. I reject categorically such polarized thinking. We can and we should help others to help themselves. But the fate of responsible men and women everywhere, in the final decision, rests in their own hands, not in ours.

America's future depends upon Americans—especially your generation, which is now equipping itself to assume the challenges of the future, to help write the agenda for America.

Earlier today, in this great community, I spoke about the need to maintain our defenses. Tonight, I would like to talk about another kind of strength, the true source of American power that transcends all of the deterrent powers for peace of our Armed Forces. I am speaking here of our belief in ourselves and our belief in our Nation.

Abraham Lincoln asked, in his own words, and I quote, "What constitutes the bulwark of our own liberty and independence?" And he answered, "It is not our frowning battlements or bristling seacoasts, our Army or our Navy. Our defense is in the spirit which prized liberty as the heritage of all men, in all lands everywhere."

It is in this spirit that we must now move beyond the discords of the past decade. It is in this spirit that I ask you to join me in writing an agenda for the future.

I welcome your invitation particularly tonight, because I know it is at Tulane and other centers of thought throughout our great country that much consideration is being given to the kind of future Americans want and, just as importantly, will work for. Each of you are preparing yourselves for the future, and I am deeply interested in your preparations and your opinions and your goals. However, tonight, with your indulgence, let me share with you my own views.

I envision a creative program that goes as

far as our courage and our capacities can take us, both at home and abroad. My goal is for a cooperative world at peace, using its resources to build, not to destroy.

As President, I am determined to offer leadership to overcome our current economic problems. My goal is for jobs for all who want to work and economic opportunity for all who want to achieve.

I am determined to seek self-sufficiency in energy as an urgent national priority. My goal is to make America independent of foreign energy sources by 1985.

Of course, I will pursue interdependence with other nations and a reformed international economic system. My goal is for a world in which consuming and producing nations achieve a working balance.

I will address the humanitarian issues of hunger and famine, of health and of healing. My goal is to achieve—or to assure basic needs and an effective system to achieve this result.

I recognize the need for technology that enriches life while preserving our natural environment. My goal is to stimulate productivity, but use technology to redeem, not to destroy our environment.

"Once social change begins, it cannot be reversed. You cannot uneducate the person who has learned to read. You cannot humiliate the person who feels pride. You cannot oppress the people who are not afraid anymore. We have seen the future, and the future is ours."

—CESAR CHAVEZ (1927–1993)
Community Organizer and Founder of the United Farm Workers of America

I will strive for new cooperation rather than conflict in the peaceful exploration of our oceans and our space. My goal is to use resources for peaceful progress rather than war and destruction.

Let America symbolize humanity's struggle to conquer nature and master technology. The time has now come for our Government to facilitate the individual's control over his or her future—and of the future of America.

But the future requires more than Americans congratulating themselves on how much we know and how many products that we can produce. It requires new knowledge to meet new problems. We must not only be motivated to build a better America, we must know how to do it.

If we really want a humane America that will, for instance, contribute to the alleviation of the world's hunger, we must realize that good intentions do not feed people. Some problems, as anyone who served in the Congress knows, are complex. There are no easy answers. Willpower alone does not grow food. We thought, in a well-intentioned past, that we could export our technology lock, stock, and barrel to developing nations. We did it with the best of intentions. But we are now learning that a strain of rice that grows in one place will not grow in another; that factories that produce at 100 percent in one nation produce less than half as much in a society where temperaments and work habits are somewhat different.

Yet, the world economy has become interdependent. Not only food technology but money management, natural resources and energy, research and development—all kinds of this group require an organized world society that makes the maximum effective use of the world's resources.

I want to tell the world: Let's grow food together, but let's also learn more about nutrition, about weather forecasting, about irrigation, about the many other specialties involved in helping people to help themselves.

We must learn more about people, about the development of communities, architecture, engineering, education, motivation, productivity, public health and medicine, arts and sciences, political, legal, and social organization. All of these specialties and many, many more are required if young people like you are to help this Nation develop an agenda for our future—your future, our country's future.

America's leadership is essential. America's resources are vast. America's opportunities are unprecedented.

As we strive together to prefect a new agenda, I put high on the list of important points the maintenance of alliances and partnerships with other people and other nations. These do provide a basis of shared values, even as we stand up with determination for what we believe. This, of course, requires a continuing commitment to peace and a determination to use our good offices wherever possible to promote better relations between nations of this world.

The new agenda, that which is developed by you and by us, must place a high priority on the need to stop the spread of nuclear weapons and to work for the mutual reduction in strategic arms and control of other weapons. And I must say, parenthetically, the successful negotiations at Vladivostok, in my opinion, are just a beginning.

Your generation of Americans is uniquely endowed by history to give new meaning to the pride and spirit of America. The magnetism of an American society, confident of its own strength, will attract the good will and the esteem of all people wherever they might be in this globe in which we live. It will enhance our own perception of ourselves and our pride in being an American. We can, we—and I say it with emphasis—write a new agenda for our future.

I am glad that Tulane University and other great American educational institutions are reaching out to others in programs to work with developing nations, and I look forward with confidence to your participation in every aspect of America's future.

And I urge Americans of all ages to unite in this Bicentennial year, to take responsibility for themselves as our ancestors did. Let us resolve tonight to rediscover the old virtues of confidence and self-reliance and capability that characterized our forefathers two centuries ago. I pledge, as I know you do, each one of us, to do our part.

Let the beacon light of the past shine forth from historic New Orleans and from Tulane University and from every other corner of this land to illuminate a boundless future for all Americans and a peace for all mankind.

Thank you very much.

RONALD REAGAN

(1911–2004)

---

*"Above all, we must realize that no arsenal,
or no weapon in the arsenals of the world, is
so formidable as the will and moral courage
of free men and women. It is a weapon our
adversaries in today's world do not have."*

Ronald Reagan was our nation's 40th President. He served for two terms, during which he brought about many political and economic changes including deregulation, tax cuts, and the overseeing of foreign affairs including ending the Cold War.

RONALD REAGAN
TEAR DOWN THIS WALL

ON THE 750TH ANNIVERSARY OF BERLIN, President Ronald Reagan stood at the Brandenburg Gate in West Berlin and urged Soviet leader Mikhail Gorbachev to "tear down" the Berlin Wall and work towards establishing peace between the Soviet Union and Eastern Europe. Although the importance of Reagan's speech was not initially recognized, his words have since become a symbol of the United States' role in ending the Cold War, while also signifying our nation's dedication to peaceful international policies.

JUNE 12, 1987

Thank you very much.

Chancellor Kohl, Governing Mayor Diepgen, ladies and gentlemen: Twenty-four years ago, President John F. Kennedy visited Berlin, speaking to the people of this city and the world at the City Hall. Well, since then two other Presidents have come, each in his turn, to Berlin. And today I, myself, make my second visit to your city.

We come to Berlin, we American Presidents, because it's our duty to speak, in this place, of freedom. But I must confess, we're drawn here by other things as well: by the feeling of history in this city, more than 500 years older than our own nation; by the beauty of the Grunewald and the Tiergarten; most of all, by your courage and determination. Perhaps the composer Paul Lincke understood something about American Presidents. You see, like so many Presidents before me, I come here today because wherever I go, whatever I do: Ich hab noch einen Koffer in Berlin. [I still have a suitcase in Berlin.]

Our gathering today is being broadcast throughout Western Europe and North America. I understand that it is being seen and heard as well in the East. To those listening throughout Eastern Europe, a special word: Although I cannot be with you, I address my remarks to you just as surely as to those standing here before me. For I join you, as I join your fellow countrymen in the West, in this firm, this unalterable belief: Es gibt nur ein Berlin. [There is only one Berlin.]

Behind me stands a wall that encircles the free sectors of this city, part of a vast system of barriers that divides the entire continent of Europe. From the Baltic, south, those barriers cut across Germany in a gash of barbed wire, concrete, dog runs, and guard towers. Farther south, there may be no visible, no obvious wall. But there remain armed guards and checkpoints all the same—still a restriction on the right to travel, still an instrument to impose upon ordinary men and women the will of a totalitarian state. Yet it is here in Berlin where the wall emerges most clearly; here, cutting across your city, where the news photo and the television screen have imprinted this brutal division of a continent upon the mind of the world. Standing before the Brandenburg Gate, every man is a German, separated from his fellow men. Every man is a Berliner, forced to look upon a scar.

President von Weizsacker has said, "The German question is open as long as the Brandenburg Gate is closed." Today I say: As long as the gate is closed, as long as this scar of a wall is permitted to stand, it is not the

German question alone that remains open, but the question of freedom for all mankind. Yet I do not come here to lament. For I find in Berlin a message of hope, even in the shadow of this wall, a message of triumph.

In this season of spring in 1945, the people of Berlin emerged from their air-raid shelters to find devastation. Thousands of miles away, the people of the United States reached out to help. And in 1947 Secretary of State—as you've been told—George Marshall announced the creation of what would become known as the Marshall Plan. Speaking precisely 40 years ago this month, he said: "Our policy is directed not against any country or doctrine, but against hunger, poverty, desperation, and chaos."

In the Reichstag a few moments ago, I saw a display commemorating this 40th anniversary of the Marshall Plan. I was struck by the sign on a burnt-out, gutted structure that was being rebuilt. I understand that Berliners of my own generation can remember seeing signs like it dotted throughout the western sectors of the city. The sign read simply: "The Marshall Plan is helping here to strengthen the free world." A strong, free world in the West, that dream became real. Japan rose from ruin to become an economic giant. Italy, France, Belgium—virtually every nation in Western Europe saw political and economic rebirth; the European Community was founded.

In West Germany and here in Berlin, there took place an economic miracle, the Wirtschaftswunder. Adenauer, Erhard, Reuter, and other leaders understood the practical importance of liberty—that just as truth can flourish only when the journalist is given freedom of speech, so prosperity can come about only when the farmer and businessman enjoy economic freedom. The German leaders reduced tariffs, expanded free trade, lowered taxes. From 1950 to 1960 alone, the standard of living in West Germany and Berlin doubled.

Where four decades ago there was rubble, today in West Berlin there is the greatest industrial output of any city in Germany— busy office blocks, fine homes and apartments, proud avenues, and the spreading lawns of parkland. Where a city's culture seemed to have been destroyed, today there are two great universities, orchestras and an opera, countless theaters, and museums. Where there was want, today there's abundance—food, clothing, automobiles—the wonderful goods of the Ku'damm. From devastation, from utter ruin, you Berliners have, in freedom, rebuilt a city that once again ranks as one of the greatest on earth. The Soviets may have had other plans. But my friends, there were a few things the Soviets didn't count on—Berliner Herz, Berliner Humor, ja, und Berliner Schnauze. [Berliner heart, Berliner humor, yes, and a Berliner Schnauze.]

In the 1950s, Khrushchev predicted: "We will bury you." But in the West today, we see a free world that has achieved a level of prosperity and well-being unprecedented in all human history. In the Communist world, we see failure, technological backwardness, declining standards of health, even want of the most basic kind—too little food. Even today, the Soviet Union still cannot feed itself. After these four decades, then, there stands before the entire world one great and inescapable conclusion: Freedom leads to prosperity. Freedom replaces the ancient hatreds among the nations with comity and peace. Freedom is the victor.

And now the Soviets themselves may, in a limited way, be coming to understand the importance of freedom. We hear much from Moscow about a new policy of reform and openness. Some political prisoners have been released. Certain foreign news broadcasts are no longer being jammed. Some economic enterprises have been permitted to operate with greater freedom from state control.

Are these the beginnings of profound changes in the Soviet state? Or are they token gestures, intended to raise false hopes in the West, or to strengthen the Soviet system without changing it? We welcome change and openness; for we believe that freedom and security go together, that the advance of human liberty can only strengthen the cause of world peace. There is one sign the Soviets can make that would be unmistakable, that would advance dramatically the cause of freedom and peace.

General Secretary Gorbachev, if you seek peace, if you seek prosperity for the Soviet Union and Eastern Europe, if you seek liberalization: Come here to this gate! Mr. Gorbachev, open this gate! Mr. Gorbachev, tear down this wall!

I understand the fear of war and the pain of division that afflict this continent—and I pledge to you my country's efforts to help overcome these burdens. To be sure, we in the West must resist Soviet expansion. So we must maintain defenses of unassailable strength. Yet we seek peace; so we must strive to reduce arms on both sides.

Beginning 10 years ago, the Soviets challenged the Western alliance with a grave new threat, hundreds of new and more deadly SS-20 nuclear missiles, capable of striking every capital in Europe. The Western alliance responded by committing itself to a counter-deployment unless the Soviets agreed to negotiate a better solution; namely, the elimination of such weapons on both sides. For many months, the Soviets refused to bargain in earnestness. As the alliance, in turn, prepared to go forward with its counter-deployment, there were difficult days—days of protests like those during my 1982 visit to this city—and the Soviets later walked away from the table.

But through it all, the alliance held firm. And I invite those who protested then—I invite those who protest today—to mark this fact: Because we remained strong, the Soviets came back to the table. And because we remained strong, today we have within reach the possibility, not merely of limiting the growth of arms, but of eliminating, for the first time, an entire class of nuclear weapons from the face of the earth.

As I speak, NATO ministers are meeting in Iceland to review the progress of our proposals for eliminating these weapons. At the talks in Geneva, we have also proposed deep cuts in strategic offensive weapons. And the Western allies have likewise made far-reaching proposals to reduce the danger of conventional war and to place a total ban on chemical weapons.

While we pursue these arms reductions, I pledge to you that we will maintain the capacity to deter Soviet aggression at any level at which it might occur. And in cooperation with many of our allies, the United States is pursuing the Strategic Defense Initiative—research to base deterrence not on the threat of offensive retaliation, but on defenses that truly defend; on systems, in short, that will not target populations, but shield them. By these means we seek to increase the safety of Europe and all the world. But we must remember a crucial fact: East and West do not mistrust each other because we are armed; we are armed because we mistrust each other. And our differences are not about weapons but about liberty. When President Kennedy spoke at the City Hall those 24 years ago, freedom was encircled, Berlin was under siege. And today, despite all the pressures upon this city, Berlin stands secure in its liberty. And freedom itself is transforming the globe.

In the Philippines, in South and Central America, democracy has been given a rebirth. Throughout the Pacific, free markets are working miracle after miracle of economic growth. In the industrialized nations, a technological revolution is taking place—a revolution marked by rapid, dramatic advances in computers and telecommunications.

In Europe, only one nation and those it controls refuse to join the community of freedom. Yet in this age of redoubled economic growth, of information and innovation, the Soviet Union faces a choice: It must make fundamental changes, or it will become obsolete.

Today thus represents a moment of hope. We in the West stand ready to cooperate with the East to promote true openness, to break down barriers that separate people, to create a safe, freer world. And surely there is no better place than Berlin, the meeting place of

East and West, to make a start. Free people of Berlin: Today, as in the past, the United States stands for the strict observance and full implementation of all parts of the Four Power Agreement of 1971. Let us use this occasion, the 750th anniversary of this city, to usher in a new era, to seek a still fuller, richer life for the Berlin of the future. Together, let us maintain and develop the ties between the Federal Republic and the Western sectors of Berlin, which is permitted by the 1971 agreement.

And I invite Mr. Gorbachev: Let us work to bring the Eastern and Western parts of the city closer together, so that all the inhabitants of all Berlin can enjoy the benefits that come with life in one of the great cities of the world.

To open Berlin still further to all Europe, East and West, let us expand the vital air access to this city, finding ways of making commercial air service to Berlin more convenient, more comfortable, and more economical. We look to the day when West Berlin can become one of the chief aviation hubs in all central Europe.

With our French and British partners, the United States is prepared to help bring international meetings to Berlin. It would be only fitting for Berlin to serve as the site of United Nations meetings, or world conferences on human rights and arms control or other issues that call for international cooperation.

There is no better way to establish hope for the future than to enlighten young minds, and we would be honored to sponsor summer youth exchanges, cultural events, and other programs for young Berliners from the East. Our French and British friends, I'm certain, will do the same. And it's my hope that an authority can be found in East Berlin to sponsor visits from young people of the Western sectors.

One final proposal, one close to my heart: Sport represents a source of enjoyment and ennoblement, and you may have noted that the Republic of Korea—South Korea—has offered to permit certain events of the 1988 Olympics to take place in the North. International sports competitions of all kinds could take place in both parts of this city. And what better way to demonstrate to the world the openness of this city than to offer in some future year to hold the Olympic games here in Berlin, East and West? In these four decades, as I have said, you

Berliners have built a great city. You've done so in spite of threats—the Soviet attempts to impose the East-mark, the blockade. Today the city thrives in spite of the challenges implicit in the very presence of this wall. What keeps you here? Certainly there's a great deal to be said for your fortitude, for your defiant courage. But I believe there's something deeper, something that involves Berlin's whole look and feel and way of life—not mere sentiment. No one could live long in Berlin without being completely disabused of illusions. Something instead, that has seen the difficulties of life in Berlin but chose to accept them, that continues to build this good and proud city in contrast to a surrounding totalitarian presence that refuses to release human energies or aspirations. Something that speaks with a powerful voice of affirmation, that says yes to this city, yes to the future, yes to freedom. In a word, I would submit that what keeps you in Berlin is love—love both profound and abiding.

Perhaps this gets to the root of the matter, to the most fundamental distinction of all between East and West. The totalitarian world produces backwardness because it does such violence to the spirit, thwarting the human impulse to create, to enjoy, to worship. The totalitarian world finds even symbols of love and of worship an affront. Years ago, before the East Germans began rebuilding their churches, they erected a secular struc- ture: the television tower at Alexander Platz. Virtually ever since, the authorities have been working to correct what they view as the tower's one major flaw, treating the glass sphere at the top with paints and chemicals of every kind. Yet even today when the sun strikes that sphere—that sphere that towers over all Berlin—the light makes the sign of the cross. There in Berlin, like the city itself, symbols of love, symbols of worship, cannot be suppressed.

As I looked out a moment ago from the Reichstag, that embodiment of German unity, I noticed words crudely spray-painted upon the wall, perhaps by a young Berliner: "This wall will fall. Beliefs become reality." Yes, across Europe, this wall will fall. For it cannot with- stand faith; it cannot withstand truth. The wall cannot withstand freedom.

And I would like, before I close, to say one word. I have read, and I have been questioned since I've been here about certain demonstrations against my coming. And I would like to say just one thing, and to those who demonstrate so. I wonder if they have ever asked themselves that if they should have the kind of government they apparently seek, no one would ever be able to do what they're doing again.

Thank you and God bless you all.

V

Traditions and Customs
of the United States

"My country, 'tis of thee,
Sweet land of liberty,
Of thee I sing;
Land where my fathers died,
Land of the pilgrims' pride,
From every mountainside
Let freedom ring!"

—excerpt from "My Country, 'Tis of Thee," American patriotic song written by Samuel Francis Smith in 1831

FOR MANY CULTURES, tradition encourages awareness of shared history. Traditions includes holidays, which commemorate an important day in history or honor an influential person or group of people. Customs play an important role in upholding and honoring a population's shared identity and often represent predominant values and sentiments.

The United States is very unique because our nation is home to people from across the globe. Each one of us is free to celebrate our own unique background with our own traditions, holidays and customs. Throughout the year, a variety of holidays honor America's diverse population. In addition, we celebrate key historical moments in our country's history on patriotic holidays. In many ways, our traditions and customs help us honor our diversity as well as celebrate our unity and equality as American citizens.

THE GREAT SEAL OF THE UNITED STATES OF AMERICA

THE GREAT SEAL WAS COMMISSIONED by the Continental Congress in 1776. The Seal has two sides. The front side features a bald eagle, the national bird. In its beak, the eagle holds a scroll inscribed *E pluribus unum* (Latin for "out of many, one") in its beak. In its claws, the eagle clutches an olive branch (signifying peace) and a bundle of thirteen arrows (signifying the military strength of the thirteen colonies). A shield covering the eagle's breast bears the red and white stripes of the nation's flag, and above the eagle's head is a cloud of thirteen stars.

The reverse side features a thirteen-step pyramid with the year 1776 in Roman numerals at its base. Above the pyramid is the Eye of Providence and the motto *Annuit Coeptis*, meaning "He [God] favors our undertakings." *Novus Ordo Seclorum* ("New Order of the Ages") is written on a scroll below the pyramid beginning of a new era in government.

1776

E PLURIBUS UNUM

(OUT OF MANY, ONE)

———————————

1956

IN GOD WE TRUST

THE NATIONAL MOTTO
of
THE UNITED STATES
OF AMERICA

HISTORY. In 1776, the Founding Fathers chose the phrase *E Pluribus Unum* ("Of Many, One") as the new nation's official motto. One hundred eighty years later, in 1956, President Dwight D. Eisenhower officially established the phrase, "In God We Trust," as the national motto of the United States. The phrase had been appearing on American currency since the end of the Civil War.

THE STAR-SPANGLED BANNER

*Oh, say, can you see, by the dawn's
early light,*

*What so proudly we hailed at the
twilight's last gleaming?*

*Whose broad stripes and bright stars,
thro' the perilous fight;*

*O'er the ramparts we watched, were so
gallantly streaming.*

*And the rockets red glare, the bombs
bursting in air,*

*Gave proof through the night that our
flag was still there.*

*Oh, say, does that star-spangled
banner yet wave*

*O'er the land of the free and the home
of the brave?*

THE NATIONAL ANTHEM

HISTORY. The lyrics of our national anthem, *The Star-Spangled Banner*, were written by Francis Scott Key towards the end of the War of 1812 against the British. Key, a lawyer and amateur poet, was a witness to the relentless bombardment of Fort McHenry by British gunboats. The attack on the fort, which guards the port of Baltimore, lasted for more than twenty-four hours.

When the smoke cleared on the morning of September 14, 1814, Key was amazed to see the American flag still waving over the battered fort. The American forces had weathered the onslaught. Key drafted a poem on the subject, "In Defense of Fort McHenry," later setting it to the tune of a popular song, "To Anacreon in Heaven."

In 1916, Woodrow Wilson decreed that the song be played at military gatherings and its popularity grew. In 1931, *The Star-Spangled Banner* was designated the official national anthem of our country.

THE FLAG OF THE UNITED STATES

HISTORY. The American flag is called the "Star-Spangled Banner," the "Stars and Stripes," the "Red, White, and Blue," and "Old Glory."

From its original design of thirteen alternating red and white stripes (representing the thirteen original states) and a blue field with thirteen stars, the American flag has changed as the country has grown. With each state's admission, a new star has been added to the original thirteen, to the present fifty stars. The flag, in short, is a visible symbol of our nation's history.

In 1949, Congress established June 14 of each year as Flag Day, to commemorate the importance of the flag.

TRADITION AND THE FLAG CODE. The present Flag Code of the United States was adopted by the National Flag Conference in Washington, D.C., in June, 1923. It has been revised and endorsed regularly by Congress since then, most recently in 2007. The Flag Code contains very specific rules concerning the display and handling of the United States flag. These include:

TIME AND OCCASIONS FOR DISPLAY. It is the universal custom to display the flag only from sunrise to sunset on buildings and on stationary flagstaffs in the open. However, when a patriotic effect is desired, the flag may be displayed 24 hours a day if properly illuminated during the hours of darkness.

HOIST BRISKLY, LOWER SLOWLY. The flag should be hoisted briskly and lowered ceremoniously.

PROTECT IT FROM INCLEMENT WEATHER. The flag should not be displayed on days when the weather is inclement, except when an all weather flag is displayed.

DISPLAY ON ALL DAYS, INCLUDING HOLIDAYS. The flag should be displayed on all days, especially on New Year's Day, January 1; Inauguration Day, January 20; Martin Luther King, Jr. Day, third Monday in January; Lincoln's Birthday, February 12; Washington's Birthday, third Monday in February; Easter Sunday (variable); Mother's Day, second Sunday in May; Armed Forces Day, third Saturday in May; Memorial Day (half-staff until noon), the last Monday in May; Flag Day, June 14; Independence Day, July 4; Labor Day, first Monday in September; Constitution Day, September 17; Columbus Day, second

Monday in October; Navy Day, October 27; Veterans Day, November 11; Thanksgiving Day, fourth Thursday in November; Christmas Day, December 25; and such other days as may be proclaimed by the President of the United States; the birthdays of States (date of admission); and on State holidays.

DISPLAY OUTSIDE PUBLIC INSTITUTIONS. The flag should be displayed daily on or near the main administration building of every public institution.

DISPLAY NEAR POLLING PLACES ON ELECTION **days.** The flag should be displayed in or near every polling place on election days.

DISPLAY NEAR SCHOOLS. The flag should be displayed during school days in or near every schoolhouse.

POSITION AND MANNER OF DISPLAY

FRONT AND CENTER. The flag, when carried in a procession with another flag or flags, should be either on the marching right; that is, the flag's own right, or, if there is a line of other flags, in front of the center of that line.

NEVER ON A FLOAT EXCEPT FROM A STAFF. The flag should not be displayed on a float in a parade except from a staff.

NEVER DRAPED OVER A VEHICLE. The flag should not be draped over the hood, top, sides, or back of a vehicle or of a railroad train or a boat. When the flag is displayed on a motor-car, the staff shall be fixed firmly to the chassis or clamped to the right fender.

POSITION OF SUPERIOR PROMINENCE. No other flag or pennant should be placed above or, if on the same level, to the right of the flag of the United States of America, except during church services conducted by naval chaplains at sea, when the church pennant may be flown above the flag during church services for the personnel of the Navy. No person shall display the flag of the United Nations or any other national or international flag equal, above, or in a position of superior prominence or honor to, or in place of, the flag of the United States at any place within the United States or any Territory or possession thereof: Provided, That nothing in this section shall make unlawful the continuance of the practice heretofore followed of displaying the flag of the United Nations in a position of superior prominence or honor, and other national flags in positions of equal prominence or honor, with that of the flag of the United States at the headquarters of the United Nations.

FIRST AMONG OTHER FLAGS. The flag of the United States of America, when it is displayed with another flag against a wall from crossed staffs, should be on the right, the flag's own right, and its staff should be in front of the staff of the other flag.

CENTRAL AND HIGHEST. The flag of the United States of America should be at the center and at the highest point of the group when a number of flags of States or localities or pennants of societies are grouped and displayed from staffs.

HOISTED FIRST AND LOWERED LAST. When flags of States, cities, or localities, or pennants of societies are flown on the same halyard with the flag of the United States, the latter should always be at the peak. When the flags are flown from adjacent staffs, the flag of the United States should be hoisted first and lowered last. No such flag or pennant may be placed above the flag of the United States or to the United States flag's right.

SAME SIZE AND HEIGHT AS FOREIGN FLAGS. When flags of two or more nations are displayed, they are to be flown from separate staffs of the same height. The flags should be of approximately equal size. International usage forbids the display of the flag of one nation above that of another nation in time of peace.

Union always at peak of staff. When the flag of the United States is displayed from a staff projecting horizontally or at an angle from the window sill, balcony, or front of a building, the union of the flag should be placed at the peak of the staff unless the flag is at half-staff. When the flag is suspended over a sidewalk from a rope extending from a house to a pole at the edge of the sidewalk, the flag should be hoisted out, union first, from the building.

Union to the left. When displayed either horizontally or vertically against a wall, the union should be uppermost and to the flag's own right, that is, to the observer's left. When displayed in a window, the flag should be displayed in the same way, with the union or blue field to the left of the observer in the street.

Union to north and east. When the flag is displayed over the middle of the street, it should be suspended vertically with the union to the north in an east and west street or to the east in a north and south street.

Behind or right of speaker. When used on a speaker's platform, the flag, if displayed flat, should be displayed above and behind the speaker. When displayed from a staff in a church or public auditorium, the flag of the United States of America should hold the position of superior prominence, in advance of the audience, and in the position of honor at the clergyman's or speaker's right as he faces the audience. Any other flag so displayed should be placed on the left of the clergyman or speaker or to the right of the audience.

NEVER USED AS COVERING FOR STATUE OR MONUMENT. The flag should form a distinctive feature of the ceremony of unveiling a statue or monument, but it should never be used as the covering for the statue or monument.

AT HALF-STAFF. The flag, when flown at half-staff, should be first hoisted to the peak for an instant and then lowered to the half-staff position. The flag should be again raised to the peak before it is lowered for the day. On Memorial Day the flag should be displayed at half-staff until noon only, then raised to the top of the staff. By order of the President, the flag shall be flown at half-staff upon the death of principal figures of the United States Government and the Governor of a State, territory, or possession, as a mark of respect to their memory. In the event of the death of other officials or foreign dignitaries, the flag is to be displayed at half-staff according to Presidential instructions or orders, or in

accordance with recognized customs or practices not inconsistent with law. In the event of
the death of a present or former official of the
government of any State, territory, or possession of the United States, the Governor of that
State, territory, or possession may proclaim
that the National flag shall be flown at half-
staff. The flag shall be flown at half-staff 30
days from the death of the President or a former President; 10 days from the day of death
of the Vice President, the Chief Justice or a
retired Chief Justice of the United States, or
the Speaker of the House of Representatives;
from the day of death until interment of an
Associate Justice of the Supreme Court, a Secretary of an executive or military department,
a former Vice President, or the Governor of a
State, territory, or possession; and on the day
of death and the following day for a Member of
Congress. The flag shall be flown at half-staff
on Peace Officers Memorial Day, unless that
day is also Armed Forces Day. As used in this
subsection— the term "half-staff" means the
position of the flag when it is one-half the dis-
tance between the top and bottom of the staff;
the term "executive or military department"
means any agency listed under sections 101
and 102 of title 5, United States Code; and the
term "Member of Congress" means a Senator,

a Representative, a Delegate, or the Resident Commissioner from Puerto Rico.

DRAPED OVER A COFFIN. When the flag is used to cover a casket, it should be so placed that the union is at the head and over the left shoulder. The flag should not be lowered into the grave or allowed to touch the ground.

UNION ALWAYS TO THE LEFT. When the flag is suspended across a corridor or lobby in a building with only one main entrance, it should be suspended vertically with the union of the flag to the observer's left upon entering. If the building has more than one main entrance, the flag should be suspended vertically near the center of the corridor or lobby with the union to the north, when entrances are to the east and west or to the east when entrances are to the north and south. If there are entrances in more than two directions, the union should be to the east.

RESPECT FOR FLAG
NO DISRESPECT SHOWN. No disrespect should be shown to the flag of the United States of America; the flag should not be dipped to any person or thing. Regimental colors, State flags, and organization or institutional flags are to be dipped as a mark of honor.

UNION NEVER DOWN. The flag should never be displayed with the union down, except as a signal of dire distress in instances of extreme danger to life or property.

NEVER TOUCH THE GROUND. The flag should never touch anything beneath it, such as the ground, the floor, water, or merchandise.

ALWAYS ALOFT AND FREE. The flag should never be carried flat or horizontally, but always aloft and free.

NEVER USE AS APPAREL, BEDDING OR DRAPERY. The flag should never be used as wearing apparel, bedding, or drapery. It should never be festooned, drawn back, nor up, in folds, but always allowed to fall free. Bunting of blue, white, and red, always arranged with the blue above, the white in the middle, and the red below, should be used for covering a speaker's desk, draping the front of the platform, and for decoration in general.

NEVER PERMIT TO BE EASILY SOILED OR DAMAGED. The flag should never be fastened, displayed, used, or stored in such a manner as to permit it to be easily torn, soiled, or damaged in any way.

NEVER A CEILING COVERING. The flag should never be used as a covering for a ceiling.

No marks, drawings or words. The flag should never have placed upon it, nor on any part of it, nor attached to it any mark, insignia, letter, word, figure, design, picture, or drawing of any nature.

Never used for carrying anything. The flag should never be used as a receptacle for receiving, holding, carrying, or delivering anything.

Never used for advertising purposes. The flag should never be used for advertising purposes in any manner whatsoever. It should not be embroidered on such articles as cushions or handkerchiefs and the like, printed or otherwise impressed on paper napkins or boxes or anything that is designed for temporary use and discard. Advertising signs should not be fastened to a staff or halyard from which the flag is flown.

Flag patches and pins. No part of the flag should ever be used as a costume or athletic uniform. However, a flag patch may be affixed to the uniform of military personnel, firemen, policemen, and members of patriotic organizations. The flag represents a living country and is itself considered a living thing. Therefore, the lapel flag pin being a replica, should be worn on the left lapel near the heart.

DIGNIFIED DESTRUCTION. The flag, when it is in such condition that it is no longer a fitting emblem for display, should be destroyed in a dignified way, preferably by burning.

CONDUCT DURING HOISTING, LOWERING OR PASSING OF FLAG

FACING THE FLAG, RIGHT HAND OVER HEART. During the ceremony of hoisting or lowering the flag or when the flag is passing in a parade or in review, all persons present except those in uniform should face the flag and stand at attention with the right hand over the heart. Those present in uniform should render the military salute. When not in uniform, men should remove their headdress with their right hand and hold it at the left shoulder, the hand being over the heart. Aliens should stand at attention. The salute to the flag in a moving column should be rendered at the moment the flag passes.

PLEDGE OF ALLEGIANCE

I pledge allegiance to the Flag of the United States of America and to the Republic for which it stands, one Nation, under God, indivisible, with liberty and justice for all.

THE PLEDGE OF ALLEGIANCE

HISTORY. The original Pledge of Allegiance read: "I pledge allegiance to my Flag and the Republic for which it stands: one Nation indivisible, with Liberty and Justice for all." It was delivered by schoolchildren for the first time on Columbus Day, 1892, to commemorate the four hundredth anniversary of the discovery of America.

The Pledge of Allegiance was officially recognized by Congress in 1942. The phrase "under God" was added to the Pledge during the administration of President Dwight D. Eisenhower.

When delivering the Pledge of Allegiance, all must be standing at attention, facing the flag with the right hand over the heart. Men not in uniform should remove any nonreligious headdress with their right hand and hold it at the left shoulder, the hand being over the heart. Those in uniform should remain silent, face the flag, and render the military salute.

NATIONAL HOLIDAYS

NEW YEAR'S DAY
January 1

MARTIN LUTHER KING, JR. DAY
Third Monday in January

PRESIDENTS' DAY/WASHINGTON'S
BIRTHDAY
Third Monday in February

MEMORIAL DAY
Last Monday in May

INDEPENDENCE DAY
July 4

LABOR DAY
First Monday in September

COLUMBUS DAY
Second Monday in October

VETERANS DAY
November 11

THANKSGIVING DAY
Fourth Thursday in November

CHRISTMAS DAY
December 25

NEW YEAR'S DAY

A celebration of the new year to come takes place on New Year's Eve. On New Year's Day, some attend church, visit family and friends, or gather to watch football. Some make "New Year's resolutions," personal plans for change and improvement in the upcoming year.

MARTIN LUTHER KING, JR. DAY

Since 1986, Americans have honored this great civil rights leader by celebrating on the third Monday of January, around the time of King's Birthday on January 15th. Congress designated the Federal legal holiday to "serve as a time for Americans to reflect on the principles of racial equality and nonviolent social change espoused by Martin Luther King, Jr."

PRESIDENTS' DAY/
WASHINGTON'S BIRTHDAY

Presidents' Day originally honored George Washington's birthday (February 22), but, over the years, the theme of the holiday expanded to celebrate Abraham Lincoln (born on February 12) and other Presidents as well. In schools across the country, students often learn about the lives of Presidents Washington and Lincoln around the time of this holiday.

MEMORIAL DAY

Memorial Day honors America's fallen soldiers. Traditionally, flowers are placed on the graves of veterans and parades are held in their honor. Memorial Day also marks the beginning of summer.

INDEPENDENCE DAY

Independence Day is America's birthday, commemorating the signing of the Declaration of Independence on July 4, 1776. It was declared a federal holiday in 1941. The Fourth of July is celebrated with fireworks displays, parades, band-shell concerts, and picnics.

LABOR DAY

Labor Day, which occurs on the first Monday in September, honors American working men and women. Since the 1880s, it has also marked the end of summer.

COLUMBUS DAY

Columbus Day honors Columbus' discovery of America in 1492 and has been celebrated since 1792. In 1971, Columbus Day became a federal holiday. Today, Columbus Day is an opportunity to honor America's diverse heritage and celebrate the traditions of many native peoples.

VETERANS DAY

Like Memorial Day, Veterans Day honors America's fighting men and women and has been observed since 1938. It is celebrated on Armistice Day, the date when the treaty ending World War I was signed. Congress renamed the holiday Veterans Day in 1954.

THANKSGIVING DAY

Thanksgiving is knit deeply into the American spirit. It celebrates colonial survival and the bounty this new land offered its first immigrants. Thanksgiving commemorates a harvest festival held in 1621 in the Plymouth Colony. The colonists shared the rewards of their hard work (including fruits, vegetables, turkeys, ducks, geese, and fish) with neighboring Native Americans. Since that first Thanksgiving, the holiday has combined the traditions of the harvest festival with the importance of community and family. The traditional Thanksgiving meal is often shared with families, friends, and those in need in honor of the American spirit of giving and gratitude.

CHRISTMAS DAY

Christmas is a Christian holiday marking the birth of the Christ Child. Decorating houses and yards with lights, putting up Christmas trees, giving gifts, and sending greeting cards have become holiday traditions even for many non-Christian Americans.

REFERENCES

References listed chronologically as they appear in the text:

Declaration of Independence. [Online version accessed December 4, 2008, at http://www.archives.gov/exhibits/charters/declaration.html.]

U.S. Constitution. [Online version accessed December 4, 2008, at http://www.archives.gov/exhibits/charters/constitution.html.]

Bill of Rights. [Online version accessed December 4, 2008, at http://www.archives.gov/exhibits/charters/bill_of_rights.html.]

Lincoln, Abraham. *The Emancipation Proclamation.* [Online version accessed December 4, 2008, at http://www.archives.gov/historical-docs/document.html?doc=8&title.raw=Emancipation%20Proclamation.]

Washington's Farewell Address. New York, New York Public Library, 1935. pg. 105; 136. Courtesy of the Milstein Division of United States History, Local History & Genealogy, The New York Public Library, Astor, Lenox and Tilden Foundations. [Online version accessed

December 4, 2008, at http://www.ourdocuments.
gov/doc.php?flash=true&doc=15.]

Cady Stanton, Elizabeth. *A History of Woman
Suffrage, Vol. 1.* New York: Fowler and Wells,
1889. Print.

Robinson, Marcus, ed. Sojourner Truth's speech
at women's rights convention in Akron, Ohio, May
1851. Anti-Slavery Bugle, June 21, 1851. [Online
version accessed December 4, 2008, at http://www.
sojournertruth.org/Library/Speeches/Default.
htm#RIGHTS.]

Lincoln, Abraham. Draft of the Gettysburg
Address: Nicolay Copy, November 1863; Series 3,
General Correspondence, 1837–1897. Transcribed
and annotated by the Lincoln Studies Center,
Knox College, Galesburg, Illinois. Available
at *Abraham Lincoln Papers at the Library of
Congress*, Manuscript Division (Washington, D.C.:
American Memory Project, [2000–02]). [Online
version accessed December 4, 2008, at http://
memory.loc.gov/ammem/alhtml/alhome.html.]

Roosevelt, Franklin D. *Annual Message to
Congress, January 6, 1941.* Records of the United
States Senate; SEN 77A-H1; Record Group 46;
National Archives. [Online version accessed

December 4, 2008, at http://www.ourdocuments.gov/doc.php?flash=true&doc=70.]

Inaugural Address, Kennedy Draft, 01/17/1961; Papers of John F. Kennedy: President's Office Files, 01/20/1961–11/22/1963; John F. Kennedy Library; National Archives and Records Administration. [Online version accessed December 4, 2008, at http://www.ourdocuments.gov/doc.php?flash=true&doc=91.]

Ford, Gerald R. Address at a Tulane University Convocation. *The Gerald R. Ford Presidential Library & Museum.* [Online version accessed December 4, 2008 at http://www.fordlibrarymuseum.gov/library/speeches/750208.htm.]

Reagan, Ronald. Remarks at Brandenberg Gate, Berlin, Germany [President's Speaking Copy], 06/12/1987 (ARC Identifier: 198491); White House Office of Records Management Subject File folder SP1107 439177 (1), Collection RR-WHORM: White House Office of Records Management File Systems (White House Central Files), 01/20/1981 - 01/20/1989; Ronald Reagan Library (NLRR); National Archives and Records Administration. [Online version accessed December 4, 2008, at http://www.reagan.utexas.edu/search/speeches/speech_srch.html.]